TOWARD SOCIAL SECURITY

TOWARD
SOCIAL SECURITY

*An Explanation of the Social Security Act
and a Survey of the Larger Issues*

by

EVELINE M. BURNS
Columbia University

New York WHITTLESEY HOUSE *London*
MCGRAW-HILL BOOK COMPANY, INC.

PUBLISHED BY WHITTLESEY HOUSE
A division of the McGraw-Hill Book Company, Inc.

Printed in the United States of America by the Maple Press Co.,
York, Pa.

FOREWORD

THE object of this book is to explain what the Social Security Act means to the ordinary man or woman. Everyone has a dual stake in the Act. As an insecure or potentially insecure individual, he looks to it to increase his own security. As a member of a highly complex society he is interested in its probable effect on the general welfare. Does it achieve its objective of reducing general insecurity? Does it do so with the minimum of disturbance to the economic order. Does it require an excessive bureaucracy? How much will it cost? Who will foot the bill?

The average man is perplexed and confused by the apparently formidable complexity of the Social Security Act. Even those who have long worked in the cause of economic security are uncertain as to the value of the product of their labors. The main provisions of the Act can, however, be fairly easily disentangled, and this I have attempted to do, omitting details which concern mainly the legal expert or

v

technical administrator. The explanation of the probable social and economic consequences of the Act presents greater difficulties. It calls both for technical knowledge and for judgments involving social values. I have attempted to present the broad issues in such a way as to leave the reader to decide for himself whether he approves of this new attempt to solve the old problem of individual insecurity. Inevitably, however, my own prejudices and social values obtrude themselves. I must therefore set out these preconceptions to the best of my ability.

In the first place, I believe that it is the function of government to concern itself with the economic as well as the physical or political security of the citizen. The day has passed when the individual can be expected to provide against all the hazards to his personal economic security. The present choice is not between individual or state-assisted provision, but between various kinds of state-assisted plans. Those who regard state assistance in this field as "un-American" should therefore avoid this book.

My second belief (which some will call an illusion) is that in a democratic society voters are most likely to choose intelligently when they are fully informed as to the implications of the available alternatives. The pursuit of mutually inconsistent ends is all too easy in a society as complicated as our own. It is the function of the economist to use his technique to explain to those who have no time to specialize in these problems the probable economic consequences of proposed measures. The average man may reasonably ask the economist to inform him on two vitally important aspects of the Social Security Act: how the gains and losses incidental to the new law will be distributed among different social classes, and the probable effect of the law upon the efficient running of the social order viewed as a machine for supplying goods and services. Economists who refuse to state their conclusions in terms the average man can understand have no right to complain of the common susceptibility to panaceas. But being thus written for the nontechnical reader, this book will fail to satisfy the professional economist or lawyer. It lacks footnotes, legal citations, and statistics. It is unprofessionally brief. Its conclusions are innocent of the nicely balanced qualifications with which experts habitually safeguard their omniscience.

My third conviction is that reforms are not unworthy of support merely because they are incomplete. I am critical of the Social Security Act in regard both to the amount of individual security provided and to the methods of provision. I share the regret of those who hold that in 1934–1935 a great opportunity was missed for passing a more socially satisfactory Security Act. But I believe nevertheless that the Act is a great achievement. Imperfect as it is, it should be accepted as a foundation upon which, by amendment, there shall be built a law to rid this country of the disgraceful insecurity which has so long characterized it and which has merely been intensified and uncovered since 1929. Such amendment must, however, rest upon frank admission of the shortcomings of the less defensible parts of the Act lest the whole be destroyed by the part.

Social reformers have often aimed too low. They have "inched along," even at times when greater daring would, by dramatizing the possibilities, have brought them more vigorous and widespread support. Cautious measures, whose significance is perceptible only to the expert, cannot fire the imagination of the ordinary man. Yet without active public support, governmentally provided economic security has an uncertain future. Had the Social Security Act been more generous and comprehensive, its chances of enlisting the popular interest would have been greater. I do not feel, however, that the voters as a whole are yet prepared for the provision of security by radically changing the economic order. Those who deny the worthwhileness of any less drastic remedy will therefore find this book anemic and naïve.

I am gratefully conscious of my obligations to the many colleagues and friends with whom I have discussed social security problems so intensively and so long. I owe especial thanks to three people who have helped me while the book was in progress. My former student, Miss Irma Rittenhouse, formerly of the staff of the Committee on Economic Security and now instructor at New York University, has read the entire manuscript, which has been both improved and simplified as a result of her criticisms. Professor Herman Gray, of New York University, gave me invaluable counsel in the writing of Chapter XII. My colleague, Arthur R. Burns, read every part of the manuscript with a critical care for which I was, I fear, not always properly grateful at the time. Without his patience and friendly criticism it would have been difficult to have completed this book while carrying my normal teaching schedule. It is obvious that for errors and failures to accept suggestions I am alone responsible.

EVELINE M. BURNS.

New York, N. Y.,
January, 1936.

CONTENTS

xi

CONTENTS

CHAPTER SIX

xii

CONTENTS

CHAPTER TWELVE

CHAPTER THIRTEEN

APPENDIX

xiii

Toward Social Security

Chapter One

THE SEARCH FOR SECURITY

M OST men have always been insecure. The stream of goods and services upon which life depends has never flowed with unfailing regularity. During the past century or two, however, the individual has become less secure because capitalist societies have become more complex and more easily put out of balance. Four types of insecurity have now developed into problems of major social importance: insecurity due to old age, insecurity due to unemployment, insecurity due to sickness, and insecurity due to the death of a breadwinner.

The Threats to Individual Security

Old age means decreasing ability to work, especially under modern conditions of production. A lifetime of work ends in poverty or dependence unless the worker has been fortunate or skillful enough to save a sufficient sum to provide for him until he dies. People who have

3

saved, and even some who were lucky enough to own capital and so live without working while young, may make unfortunate investments and thus find themselves without income in old age. In normal times about one-third of all persons sixty-five years of age and over are dependent on others for support. In severe depressions, when older people are among the first to be fired and when small savings are destroyed by bank failures, this proportion is much greater. The risk of poverty or dependence in old age faces a great majority of the population.

Even in the years of their greatest vitality workers are exposed to the risk of poverty owing to unemployment. This risk increases rather than diminishes in importance. Somewhat more than 85 per cent of the income-receiving population must work for their living. No job means no income. It has been estimated that even in 1923 (a most favorable year for employment) 5.2 per cent of all the would-be wage and salary earners were unable to obtain work. In bad times the percentage increases greatly. In 1933 it was estimated that some 12,000,000 workers or about one-third of the wage-earning population were unsuccessfully seeking employment. Even after two years of at least faint revival and vast expenditures to create jobs the number of the incomeless unemployed was still about 10,000,000.

4

The hazard of ill health is a serious additional economic risk to the majority of the population. Medical advice and medicines cost money which must be taken from incomes often none too large, and sickness may also render individuals unable to earn any income at all. The total costs of sickness are staggering. Families with incomes of under $2,500 a year are said to spend no less than $1,500,000,000 annually on medical advice and medicines. This cost is not even spread equally. A study of families earning from $1,200 to $2,000 a year in 1928 to 1931 showed that out of every 1,000 persons, 218 had medical bills of more than $100, 80 had to pay more than $200, while 16 of the 80 had to meet bills ranging from $400 to $700.

Wage earners lose on the average about seven days of work a year because of illness, a serious matter when we consider the size of the average wage earner's income. Sickness strikes unequally in this respect also. Nearly one-half of the entire population suffer no illness requiring medical treatment in any given year. But about one-eighth of the population lose every year something less than one week's work through sickness, while another eighth are too ill to work for anywhere from 1 to 52 weeks. Some are never able to obtain work again. Many thousands are disabled by accidents or by physical infirmities such as blindness or the loss of use of their limbs.

Many millions of the population depend during many years of their lives upon the earnings of others. Children and housewives lose their frail security if their breadwinners die or are unable to earn. In 1930 there were 4,700,000 widows in the United States of whom 40 per cent were sixty-five years of age or over and 82 per cent forty-five or over. Such women have a slim chance of obtaining paid employment in a world that has little use for older and inexperienced people. There are about 2,000,000 widows in the country with dependent children, and at the end of 1934 more than 700,000 children receiving aid from the Federal Emergency Relief Administration came from families in which there was no breadwinner.

The Social Security Act

The Social Security Act has been passed with the object of lessening this shocking insecurity. It has been hailed as "affording protection against the loss of income due to unemployment, old age and the death of the breadwinner," and as laying the foundation stone "in a security structure which aims to protect our people against the major hazards of life." If it protects

6

the individual against these four main hazards to his security, it is indeed an achievement deservedly regarded as "a milestone in our progress toward a better ordered society." But does it?

This formidable and confusing Act occupies 32 pages and is divided into 11 involved parts. Sorting out the various sections reveals that some action has been taken in each of the four fields of insecurity. The federal government establishes a fund to provide annuities as a right to certain people when they are over sixty-five. It obtains the necessary money by taxing employers on their payrolls and workers on their wages or salaries. It encourages the states to provide more adequate assistance in the form of old-age pensions for needy people to whom its annuity plan does not apply and to annuitants who can prove that they are still in need.

The Act seeks to provide against unemployment by encouraging the states to set up so-called unemployment compensation plans providing cash benefits as a right to unemployed workers.

Money is granted under the Act for general public health purposes while the states are assisted to provide health services for two groups particularly unable to provide against sickness, namely, mothers and children. Persons incapacitated from earning because of blindness may be given more adequate pensions because the federal

7

government offers to share their cost with the states. Those otherwise physically handicapped will obtain more advice and training because the Security Act provides additional money for this purpose.

The Act also recognizes the problems of dependent persons who have been deprived of their breadwinner. The federal government is empowered to offer money to states willing to grant cash incomes to those who are caring for needy dependent children. The states are also encouraged to provide various services for dependent children who have no relatives or friends who will provide them with a home.

Finally, the Act sets up a Social Security Board of three persons to administer the whole of this federal program and to study the needs of the country and the ways in which security can best be increased. For the first time a department of the federal government will devote its full time to the problems of insecurity.

The Meaning of Social Security

Will this program give security? Harry Hopkins, Federal Emergency Relief Administrator, once remarked that "there has been so much tinkering around with the term economic security, that if the people of America have a clear

8

picture of what it means, it is a marvel." His remarks are equally applicable to the term "social security." The two terms are often used interchangeably. Even the Social Security Act began life as the Economic Security Bill, as was appropriate to the child of the labors of the Committee on Economic Security. It became the Social Security Act only on its way through Congress.

The security that most people yearn for is economic security—protection against the hazards that threaten income. But social security, or security for society as a whole, means something more than this. Social security is achieved when the economic security of the individual is assured in ways that commend themselves to the mass of the community as being just and fair, and which disturb the smooth running of our economic order as little as possible. One of the main objects of this book will be to examine the Act from this point of view in order to discover whether it meets these tests of true social security.

Three obvious questions will be asked concerning the Social Security Act by those who hope to benefit from it. They will want to know how much security it will provide, how many people will obtain this security, and who will pay for it. The first of these questions has many aspects.

9

Insecure people will want to know whether the security afforded by the Act is any improvement on the kind of assistance given in the past through the public welfare system. Will it take the form of services or cash? If the latter, how much income can an individual count upon? Will it be adjusted to the size of his family? How long will it last? Under what conditions will it be paid? Will he obtain it as a right or as a grudging concession? Will it be denied him until he is penniless? What price in terms of loss of social prestige must he pay for it?

A brief glance at the Act explains the importance of the second question as to who gets the newly available security, for almost every section excludes certain people from benefits. The average man will want to know whether in order to obtain security he will have to live in certain states or work at specified employments, or whether it will be his regardless of his place of residence or type of employer.

It is of vital importance to insecure people to know who must pay the bill for increased security. The Act adopts various financial devices and levies new taxes, the meaning of which is difficult to discover. Nevertheless, we must face the pointed questions likely to be asked by those who hope to benefit from the Act. Is the involved financial machinery merely a roundabout way of compelling each worker to pay for his own security? Will he also pay for that of anyone else? Will other people contribute toward the cost of his security?

Interest in the answer to these three basic questions is not confined to those who hope to benefit directly from the Act. Society as a whole has a stake in the extent and nature of the benefits resulting from the Social Security Act. Different ways of giving security have different effects upon the willingness of people to work and save. Some kinds of security may be so inadequate and distasteful to those to whom they are offered that the very stability of our economic order is threatened by the existence of a large body of dissatisfied and desperate citizens. Some ways of giving security disturb our economic order more than others because they interfere to a greater extent with the play of private enterprise.

The scope of the security given by the Act has also its social aspect. The Act will bring into existence vast administrative machines not only in Washington but also throughout the states. It involves the collection of tremendous taxes, and will put thousands of people to a great deal of inconvenience, if nothing worse. It is important, therefore, to ask how much advantage in the form of increased social security results from all this elaborate organization and increased taxation. Is the Act "full of sound and fury, signifying nothing" of any consequence? If it excludes many people from its benefits, are these exclusions, which reduce the social significance of the Act, reasonable or inevitable? If but a few people benefit, will the Act be worth the irritation, ill will, and sacrifice that it will occasion?

The question as to who finally pays for such additional security as the Act provides is likewise a matter of social and not merely individual concern. The collection of money to finance economic security has economic repercussions. How will the imposition of increased taxes on employers or workers or other groups in the community affect production? Are there some methods of collecting the money which are less harmful than others? From the social point of view it is also important to know whether, if some people obtain security for which they have not paid, the burden is placed upon the strongest or the weakest shoulders. If it is placed in the main upon those in the lower income groups, so that the poor support the poor, this distribution of the cost may not conform to our ideas of social justice. Immediate economic security may lead to ultimate social insecurity if many people feel that the distribution of the cost is unjust.

The first step toward answering these questions which vitally concern both insecure individuals and society as a whole is to ask what kind of security the Act provides, who obtains it, and who pays for it in each of the four major fields of insecurity.

Chapter Two

OLD-AGE SECURITY AS A RIGHT

THE Social Security Act attempts to reduce the insecurity of old people in two ways. It sets up a federal plan to guarantee annuities to people over sixty-five in return for the payment of contributions: it also tries to encourage states to provide assistance to the needy aged who do not benefit from the first plan, or who receive under it annuities too small to live upon. It is very important to be clear about the difference between these two methods. The one gives cash *annuities* (called Old-Age Benefits) as a right to all aged workers who have contributed toward their cost. The other provides cash *pensions* (called Old-Age Assistance) to old people over sixty-five if they are in need and whether or not they were previously workers.

The annuity, being in the nature of a contract between the contributing worker and the federal government, belongs absolutely to the annuitant, who can spend it just as he wishes or save it to bequeath to his heirs. The pension is a form of

14

public welfare, paid as a concession and not as a right, and can be claimed back by the state out of any property the aged person may leave when he dies. The annuity plan is paid for by taxes on employers and workers. The old-age assistance pensions are paid for out of general taxation levied by the federal and state governments. The contributory annuity plan is a nationwide scheme, applying equally to the citizens of all states, unless they work in certain industries or employments. The old-age assistance is a state plan which will benefit aged people only in those states which pass the necessary laws. These two ways of giving security to the aged are so different that we must discuss them separately. In this chapter we shall deal only with the annuity plan.

Old-age Annuities

The essence of the benefits or contributory plan is that it gives people a right to an income in the future. The federal government compels all employers and workers in certain trades to pay taxes or contributions from January 1, 1937, in return for which it promises to pay annuities to workers when they are over sixty-five. Hitherto, the government has attempted to compel workers and employers to contribute to a retirement fund only in the case of the railroad employees. In 1934 the Railroad Employees Retirement Act required employers and workers to contribute to a fund out of which annuities were to be paid as a right to retired railroad employees on reaching the age of sixty-five. This Act was declared unconstitutional in 1935. It was immediately replaced by another, which attempted to meet the technical objections of the Supreme Court, but retained the essential feature of an annuity plan financed by contributions from employers and workers. The Social Security Act extends this type of old-age security to a wider circle of workers.

What Kind of Security?

The amount of the annuity will vary from $10 to $85 a month. It will be equal to a certain percentage of a worker's total earnings from the day the system comes into effect until the time he is sixty-five. It will thus depend upon the number of years he has contributed and how high his wages have been. But the lower paid workers and those who have paid the tax a relatively short time get favorable treatment as compared with the higher paid and longer employed workers. In the first place, however much a man earns, and even if he works every year of his

16

life until he is sixty-five, he cannot get an
annuity of more than $85. Secondly, in calculat-
ing a man's total earnings in the course of his
working life, no account is taken of any sum
over $3,000 earned by him in any one year.
And finally, although the annuities are calculated
as a percentage of a man's total earnings, a
smaller percentage is allowed on higher than
on lower incomes.

If during the whole period in which a worker
has been in employment the total sum received
by him in remuneration is not more than
$3,000 (which would normally happen only if
he was already quite old when he began to
contribute) he will obtain a monthly annuity
equal to ½ of 1 per cent of his total earnings.
If he has received in wages a total sum amounting to more than $3,000, he will get an annuity
equal to ½ of 1 per cent of the first $3,000 plus
$\frac{1}{12}$ of 1 per cent of the remainder up to $45,000,
plus only $\frac{1}{24}$ of 1 per cent of any amount over
$45,000. No annuity will be paid to anyone
whose total earnings are less than $2,000.

We can see what this means if we consider the
case of a man earning $100 a month, who starts
to insure as a young man and who in the course
of his working life pays contributions for 40
years. His annual income will be $1,200, and his
total wages for 40 years will be $48,000. His

monthly annuity will then be $51.25, calculated as shown below:

$\frac{1}{2}$ of 1 per cent of the first $ 3,000 = $15.00
$\frac{1}{12}$ of 1 per cent of the next   42,000 =   35.00
$\frac{1}{24}$ of 1 per cent of the next   3,000 =   1.25
                                                  ———
                                                 $51.25

On the other hand the total earnings of a man earning $250 a month, who had contributed for 45 years, would be $135,000. At first sight it would seem that he ought to be entitled to an annuity of $87.50, calculated as follows:

$\frac{1}{2}$ of 1 per cent of the first $ 3,000 = $15.00
$\frac{1}{12}$ of 1 per cent of the next   42,000 =   35.00
$\frac{1}{24}$ of 1 per cent of the next   90,000 =   37.50
                                                  ———
                                                 $87.50

But he will obtain an annuity of only $85 because this is the maximum amount permitted under the Act. The amount of the annuities that can be obtained by workers earning various sums of money and contributing for varying periods is shown in the table on page 19.

Because the amount of the annuity depends both on the level of wages and the number of years of contribution, a worker earning $200 a month has to work for only 10 years in order to become entitled to the same annuity as a man who earns only $50 a month but works for 40 years.

ILLUSTRATIVE MONTHLY BENEFITS

Average monthly earnings, dollars	Years of employment				
	10	20	30	40	45
50	$17.50	$22.50	$27.50	$32.50	$35.00
100	22.50	32.50	42.50	51.25	53.75
150	27.50	42.50	53.75	61.25	65.00
200	32.50	51.25	61.25	71.25	76.25
250	37.50	56.25	68.75	81.25	85.00

Thus the Social Security Act guarantees to aged people, in return for the wage taxes paid when they were younger, an income of between $10 and $85 a month for as long as they live. They will obtain this income as a right and not as a charitable gift which can be withheld at any time. No one will inquire how much other income they possess or whether they have any savings. In this respect the payments are quite different from the pensions which in the past have been paid to needy aged people in a number of states. Yet these annuities are not exactly similar to those which people could obtain by paying contributions to a private company; for in order to obtain his annuity at sixty-five a

19

man must give up his job. He loses his right to his annuity for every month that he works.

This condition conflicts with the idea of a contract which, as we saw, was the very essence of this kind of annuity in contrast with the old-age assistance hitherto given. Why should a worker who has regularly paid contributions not be permitted to run his private life as he wishes after the age of sixty-five? The object of imposing this condition was to compel older people to give up their jobs in favor of the young. But it is questionable whether it is fair to use the contributory annuities system for this purpose, especially since the annuities to be paid to older people in the years immediately ahead will be very small.

As with all insurance schemes, a worker must satisfy certain conditions to obtain the annuity. First of all he must, as we have seen, be over sixty-five years of age. Secondly, the total wages on which he has paid the wage tax must amount to not less than $2,000. In the third place, a contributing worker must have been employed for wages and must have paid contributions on at least one day in each of five different calendar years between the introduction of the plan and the day on which he reached the age of sixty-five.

The kind and amount of security given by the federal old-age annuity plan has been frequently misunderstood. It is therefore important to notice that, whatever happens, every worker will obtain back all his contributions together with a further ½ of 1 per cent of his total earnings in lieu of interest on his contributions. If when he is sixty-five he fails to satisfy all the conditions qualifying for an annuity, he will not lose the money he paid in. If, for example, he has paid the wage tax on different occasions but the total sum on which he paid amounts to less than $2,000, he will be sure of getting back the 3½ per cent of the sum on which he actually paid taxes. If he dies before the age of sixty-five, this sum will be paid as a death benefit. If he dies after sixty-five but before he has drawn in annuities a sum equal to 3½ per cent of his total earnings, the difference between this sum and what he actually drew will be paid to his estate. Thus the plan is really a compulsory savings plan with insurance features for those who live long enough. In a later section we shall have to ask who pays for the benefits obtained by people who live so long that they draw out of the fund annuities amounting to more than they have paid in.

The second point to notice about the annuity plan is that while the government puts a limit of $85 a month to the annuities to be paid under the Security Act, there is nothing to prevent employers who desire to make more generous provision for their workers from so doing. When the Bill was before Congress an attempt was made to amend the Act to exempt companies having their own pension plans from contributing to the federal annuity plan. This was the object of the much discussed Clark Amendment. But the more carefully the situation was studied the less necessary did such an amendment seem to be.

Those employers who desire to offer their workers even more security than the Act provides are quite free to do so. They can take out additional insurance with a private company to provide such extra benefits as they wish. If they already have plans which provide higher benefits than the federal government offers, they may use the federal plan for providing the benefits up to the levels offered by the Security Act, and finance the remainder privately. They may even gain by so doing. By paying 3 per cent of the payroll to the federal government they can obtain for their older workers a higher annuity than they could obtain for the same sum from a private insurance company.

Where the existing private plans provide less security than the federal annuities plan it would be necessary for the companies to increase the benefits at least up to the governmental level. Otherwise their workers would be at a disadvantage compared with those elsewhere and would probably seek another employer. Even the Clark Amendment proposed to allow employers to "contract out" only if their benefits were at least as good as those offered by the government. As a matter of fact, a company wishing to run its own plan would have to offer benefits considerably superior to those afforded by the Security Act, for two reasons. Firstly, unless it did so workers would prefer to be covered by the federal plan which would apply to them wherever they chose to work. Secondly, only if it offers higher benefits is there any inducement to workers to stay with the firm or feel a special obligation to it; unless it improved on the government offering, it would have all its trouble with no reward in the form of better service.

The Security Act will indeed greatly benefit employers and workers in many of the companies which have had plans in the past but which no longer wish to continue them. Many companies have not laid aside enough money to provide for the obligations when they fall due. In the period 1929–1932, 45 out of approximately 500 industrial pension plans were discontinued or suspended; in 84 others the conditions were changed to the disadvantage of the pensioners. In spite of this drastic pruning, private pension plans were in an even more precarious position in 1932 than in 1929. To make good their guarantee in future these companies will have only to make up the difference between the annuity provided by the federal government (toward which they pay their 3 per cent payroll tax) and the sum they originally promised their workers. For this reason the Security Act will not be unwelcome to many firms.

Who Can Obtain an Annuity?

Old-age annuities are provided only to people who have paid the tax on earnings. It is therefore important to discover who these contributors will be. The old-age annuities program covers every person who works for wages or salary in any part of the United States unless he happens to fall into one of the groups expressly excluded. Both the office boy earning $10 a week and the manager of the steel company recently reported to have received a salary of $350,000 a year are covered. The latter will pay taxes only on the first $3,000 of his salary, but when he is old, he will, like the office boy, be entitled to an annuity based on the sum on which he and his employer have paid the tax.

But while the Act provides secure annuities for highly paid people who might be expected to be perfectly able to provide for their own old age, it fails to provide them for a great many people whose need is only too obvious. There will be no annuities for workers in agriculture, in domestic service in a private home, or in the employment of the federal or state governments or their instrumentalities, because these groups are not allowed to contribute. Officers and members of the crews of ships, and workers engaged in casual labor which has nothing to do with their employers' trade or business, are also excluded. Finally, by a curious irony, those who are working for a good cause will, for that very reason, be denied old-age annuities: the employees of non-profit-making organizations, including religious, charitable, scientific, literary, or educational institutions, and societies for the prevention of cruelty to children or animals are also excluded from the benefits of the Act. Added to all these millions are many others who will be unable to contribute toward old-age annuities because they are not wage earners but self-employed farmers, professional men, or owners of small businesses or shops. The Act provides no annuities for those not gainfully employed, a large and often needy group. More than 24 million people obtain their living as housewives. Many people live on incomes from their own property. At all times there are thousands of widows left unprovided for by their husbands and thousands of aged people who have lost their small properties and have no other source of income. In reality this part of the Act gives security only to 25.8 million people or a little over one-half the gainfully employed population, and a little less than one-third (32.3 per cent) of the total adult population between the ages of fifteen and sixty-five.

It could hardly be claimed that all these people are left out of the annuity plan because they do not need security. Some but by no means all of the office workers in the employment of the federal and state governments, and of the teachers employed by the states, obtain pensions when they retire. By no means all the non-profit-making, charitable, and religious organizations have pension schemes for their employees, and even where these exist they frequently protect but a small proportion of the total staff. Even in such organizations as the Y.M.C.A. and the Y.W.C.A., which strongly protested against exclusion from the Act, the pension plan covers in the one case only 3,500 out of 15,500 workers, and in the other 2,600 out of some 7,000 employees. Agriculture and domestic service are among the lower paid employments, and only very rarely do aging workers in these employments receive any pensions from their employers.

These exclusions from the security given by old-age annuities affect different sections of the population in different ways. They press heavily upon two important groups, namely, women and Negroes, who are very largely employed in the occupations to which the Act does not apply. Women work as housewives, as domestic servants, and as teachers or welfare workers in the employment of federal and state governments. They work as nurses in hospitals and form a large part of the clerical staffs of federal and state governments and of the educational, charitable, and religious organizations. All these employments are excluded from the annuity plan. Women may well be much disappointed with this part of the Act. The colored population is almost as badly off. In 1930 40.7 per cent of all the gainfully employed colored men were engaged in agriculture. Of all gainfully employed colored women 62.6 per cent were in domestic or personal service, and most but not all of them were working for private employers. They also will obtain no benefits from the annuity plan. This part of the Security Act has been described as a plan to provide security for white male wage earners, and there is some truth in the charge.

To provide anything like complete security in old age the Act must be changed in the near future to take in as many as possible of the employments now excluded. These excluded people might be assisted to obtain greater security by making it easy for those who wish to do so to contribute toward annuities themselves, paying the full cost. The original Bill did indeed contain such a plan. The federal government would have been permitted to accept money from these voluntary contributors, guaranteeing them in return annuities in their old age. Such annuity certificates would have been sold only to American citizens, and yielded annuities after the age of sixty-five not exceeding $100 a month. It is no new thing for the government to make it easy for people of small means to save by providing a convenient and safe kind of investment for them. During the war it sold savings certificates to people of small means; indeed, the proposal contained in the Social Security Bill was largely modeled on the War Savings Certificate Act.

Private insurance companies by no means fully meet the needs of small savers. Their collection costs are high, and, as a result, the benefit offered is small in proportion to the payments made. The companies do not encourage the sale of such annuities and offer very few facilities. Many people would like to save for their old age but do not trust private companies. The government could sell annuity bonds at post offices which would be within reach of everyone.

By running the voluntary plan side by side with its compulsory plan, the federal government could probably give small savers better terms. It could certainly offer them greater security.

Although some of the leading insurance men in the country believed that this voluntary plan would, in the long run, have helped and not harmed the insurance companies, those who were powerful in the Washington lobbies disagreed and Congress cut out this section of the Bill.

The number of people who will obtain annuities is limited in one other way. No annuities will be paid for the first five years of the plan. Aged people will therefore obtain no additional security from this part of the Act until 1942.

Who Pays for the Annuities?

This question is not very difficult to answer. The annuities are financed out of the taxes paid by employers and workers. From 1937 onward, both groups will have to pay to the federal government 1 per cent of the total wages paid or received by them. This percentage will rise every three years. Thus, employers and workers will each pay 1½ per cent from 1940 to 1942, 2 per cent from 1943 to 1945, 2½ per cent from 1946 to 1948, and 3 per cent in 1948 and thereafter. These taxes will yield more than 1 billion dollars a year by 1943 and by the time the plan

29

has been in force for a generation, more than 2 billion dollars.

Most of the people getting annuities in the next few years will have paid contributions only for a short time and will be entitled to much less than the annuities due to the workers who contribute throughout their working lives. To begin with, therefore, in each year more money will be collected than is paid out. The balance will be used to build up a reserve or savings fund (called the Old-age Reserve Account) just as would be the case under a private savings plan. But by about 1980 all the people claiming annuities will have been paying contributions for upward of 40 years, and the sum required each year to pay them will be more than the money supplied by the annual 6 per cent tax paid by employers and workers. The difference will be met out of the interest on the reserve fund which has been piling up all these years. By 1980 this fund will be so large that if it earns interest at only 3 per cent, it will yield each year 1.4 billion dollars, or more than half as much as the yearly taxes on employers and workers.

The actuaries and economists concerned had to make certain guesses in working out the plan. They had to estimate the numbers of people who will be contributing, the length of time they will live, the number of years for which each will claim an annuity, the amount of the annuity each will be entitled to, and the yield from the combined 6 per cent tax. According to their present calculations, by about 1980 the plan should be paying for itself. The annuity payments will be roughly equal to the money coming in from the tax and from the interest on the reserve fund. But if future events falsify any of these estimates, there will be a deficit or a surplus. Since the actuaries will have tried to keep the cost as low as possible in order not to have to tax employers and workers too heavily, the estimates are more likely to be optimistic than pessimistic.

The age at which people will claim the annuity is one of the most difficult and important of these estimates. For while they are entitled to an annuity at sixty-five, workers will not get it so long as they remain at work. In other countries, where the annuity is paid to people at sixty-five whether they work or not, this problem does not arise. But under the present scheme the actuaries must guess how many people will be tempted to continue at work. They have estimated that the average age of retirement will be sixty-seven and one-half instead of sixty-five. The calculated annual cost of the annuities is thus much less than it would be if they had assumed instead that every person claimed his annuity on his sixty-fifth birthday. If they prove to be wrong in their guess (and it seems a little optimistic), the payroll taxes and interest together will not suffice to pay the cost of annuities in future years and the difference, which will amount to a very large sum, will have to be made up from some other source. Since the federal government is instructed in the Act to pay each year into the reserve account a sum of money sufficient to meet the claims of people who have contributed, any deficit must be supplied from general taxation unless the payroll taxes are increased.

The federal government may have to participate in the cost for another reason. No money is set aside in the Act to pay the costs of administration. Like the money for current benefits and for the reserve, it will have to come from the annual payroll taxes. If these costs do not amount to more than 5 per cent of the yield from the taxes at the full 6 per cent rate, enough money will be provided from employers and workers alone. If administrative costs exceed this amount the difference will have to come out of general taxation.

Whether or not the federal government will share in the cost of annuities will therefore depend upon the accuracy of the estimates on which the plan is now built. It will have to contribute only if the average worker claims his annuity before he is sixty-seven and one-half and if the money coming in annually from the payroll and wage tax is insufficient to cover the costs of current benefits plus the amount the government must put into the reserve plus the somewhat uncertain costs of administration.

The financial burden is somewhat unequally divided among the employers and workers paying the 6 per cent tax. We saw, on page 17, that the people who had been contributing the shortest period of time and who had received the lowest wages were given an annuity larger than they would be entitled to solely on the basis of what they had contributed. In other words, these people are given "unearned" annuities. But who pays for these unearned annuities? Since on the basis of existing calculations the plan is to be financed entirely by employers and workers, the cost must come out of the taxes paid by other workers and their employers. People who are in the higher income groups, or who have contributed to the fund for a relatively long time, will have to pay higher contributions in order to obtain their annuity than they would have had to pay if they were not saddled with the cost of paying the unearned annuities of the people who were already old at the time the plan was introduced. As a result, those who are in-

33

sured for only a short period, and to some extent also the lower paid workers, receive under the government's plan a larger annuity than they could have obtained from a private company in return for a 6 per cent contribution. The higher paid and longer employed workers, however, receive less.

But it cannot be said that these "unearned" annuities for some workers will be paid for directly out of the contributions of others. Each worker is assured that he will get out of the plan at least as much as he himself has paid into it: he is guaranteed the return of 3½ per cent of the total of wages on which he has paid the tax. The cost of the unearned annuity is therefore not carried by higher paid and longer employed workers out of their *own* taxes. Since the whole plan is financed only out of employers' and workers' contributions, it must come out of the employers' contributions.

The matter can be put another way by saying that the higher paid and longer employed workers will get much less than their proportionate share of the employers' contributions because part of the share that they might otherwise have obtained will be used to pay for the unearned annuities. In Chapter Nine we shall see that in the last resort a considerable proportion of the tax paid by employers is likely to be shifted on to the shoulders of workers. If this happens the higher paid and longer employed workers will indeed be bearing the cost of the unearned annuities of their fellows.

Summary

At the beginning of this chapter it was said that the Social Security Act attempted to provide economic security for the aged in two ways. It set up a federal contributory annuities plan and offered grants to the states to make possible the payment of non-contributory pensions to aged persons in need. Aged people who during their working lives have belonged to the 32.3 per cent of the adult population covered by the old-age annuities plan will be entitled to annuities ranging from $10 to $85 a month. For the next few years most of these annuities will be small since many people will reach the age of sixty-five without having had an opportunity to contribute long enough to provide a large annuity. But by the time the plan has been in force for a generation the man who has earned an average of $100 a month will be able to look forward to a monthly annuity of between $50 and $55. Since he has contributed toward the cost of this annuity, a worker can claim it as a right and can draw it as long as he lives regardless of his private means.

Large sections of the population will be denied the opportunity to obtain annuities. People who are not wage earners are not covered by the plan, nor are those working in agriculture, domestic service in a private home, or for non-profit-making organizations. A number of other employments are also excluded. Women and, to a lesser degree, colored workers are likely to benefit but little. The annuities scheme will cover a little over half of those gainfully employed and only about one-third of the total adult population. No one can obtain an annuity before 1942.

A worker will have paid for a considerable part of his own annuity in the form of a wage tax. But a larger proportion of it will come from the taxes paid by his employer and the employers of workers who died before reaching the age of sixty-five. Lower paid workers will benefit more from the taxes paid by their employers than the higher paid.

Chapter Three

OLD-AGE SECURITY AS A CONCESSION

AGED people who are not covered by the annuities plan, or who are entitled under it to annuities too small to live upon, may still hope for security in the form of old-age pensions. But unlike the annuities, these pensions will be paid to them only if they are in need and will be financed out of general taxation. Such pensions are already paid in a number of states. Through the Security Act the federal government hopes to persuade all the states in the Union to give pensions of this kind to the needy aged. It does so by offering to share in the cost if the state laws meet certain standards laid down in the Act. But the final decision as to whether they want to meet these standards and thus secure the federal funds lies in the hands of the states. Even then the federal standards still leave them free to decide within wide limits the conditions under which these pensions shall be paid and how much they shall be. It is difficult, therefore, to give any simple answer to the question: how much difference will this part of the Act make to the lives of aged people? Everything depends upon the willingness of the states to change their laws so as to qualify for the federal grants and upon the liberality of the conditions the states establish once they have accepted the minimum federal standards. We can form some idea of the kind of security that will probably be offered by studying the recent pension laws of the states.

What Kind of Security?

The assistance provided will take the form of a cash pension. The federal government grants no money to help pay the costs of maintaining people in public institutions. Aged people greatly prefer a pension to ordinary public welfare assistance because it enables them to live in familiar surroundings instead of having to enter an institution to obtain security.

The amount of the pension has been very small in most states. With four exceptions they have set legal limits to the amount of the monthly pension. These limits varied from $12.50 in North Dakota and $15 in Indiana to $35 in Florida and California, while in Alaska the pension limit for a woman was as high as $45 a month. The most usual limit is $30 a month or $1 a day. But these

38

are only upper limits. The average actual monthly payment during 1934 was only $14.69. It was as low as 69 cents in North Dakota, and as high as $26.08 in Massachusetts.

Through the Social Security Act the federal government hopes to persuade the states to pay more adequate pensions by offering to pay 50 per cent of the cost of any pension up to $30. If states pay pensions above this figure they will have to carry the additional amount themselves. The federal government will pay a further 5 per cent over and above its share of the actual pensions as a contribution toward the cost of administration.

This part of the Act has been criticized because the federal government limits its offer to $15 per month per person plus 5 per cent for administration. In fact the federal offer is not even as generous as this because the limit of $15 applies to each individual pension. Even though its average pension is $30 a person, a state will be able to claim from the federal government less than half this amount per person on the average if it pays some pensions of $20 and others of $40. Since the federal government pays 50 per cent of each pension or $15, whichever is less, the state will be entitled to a grant equal to half the $20 pension or $10, plus half the first $30 only of the $40 pension. The average grant per person from the federal government would therefore be only $12.50 (*i.e.*, $10 + $15 ÷ 2). In states where there are great differences in the cost of living between different parts of the state or where the needs of pensioners vary widely, this method of fixing the federal government's contribution may prevent the states from adjusting pensions to need. Even in New York City while the average pension in February, 1935, was $25.37, 11.25 per cent of all the pensioners were receiving $36 or more a month. Under the Security Act New York will still have to pay the whole of any sum over $30 a month.

There is, of course, nothing in the Act prohibiting the states from granting pensions above $30 a month if they wish to do so. But it is probable that they will do this only in exceptional cases, since they will obtain no help from the federal government for any pensions over $30. Yet before we criticize the Security Act for miserliness, we must remember that $30 is, as we have seen, much above the level of the pensions now paid. In order to obtain the full $15 assistance for each person from the federal government all the states would have to increase their pensions. Only 10 of the states or territories paying pensions in 1934 were paying pensions averaging above $15 a month.

Much more serious than the setting of a maximum to what the federal government will grant is the failure to set a minimum to what the states must pay to their aged. States may therefore use the federal grants not to improve the security of their aged but to save themselves money. They can pay the same pensions as before and charge the federal government with half the cost. In the hope of preventing this the Committee on Economic Security wrote certain minimum standards into the original Bill. It was laid down that a state could claim federal help only if the pension given would be large enough when added to the income of aged persons to provide "a reasonable subsistence compatible with decency and health." This requirement would have raised the pension level in many states. But, for reasons which we shall discuss later, Congress struck it out.

The Act lays down one condition that may bring about more adequate pensions. No state can get the federal money unless it pays at least some of the costs of the old-age pensions. In the past many states left it to the counties to provide the necessary funds or made them pay the major proportion of the cost. The tiny pensions paid in many counties and the absence of any pensions at all in others were largely due to this fact. During the past few years the counties have found it more and more difficult to raise money. At the same time their expenses have increased on account of growing unemployment relief expenditures. Economies have been made and often this was done at the expense of the aged.

The financial resources of the states are, however, much greater than those of the counties. In states in which all or a considerable part of the cost of the pensions has been carried by the state rather than the county, the aged have fared somewhat better. The security given to old people is likely to be a little greater, therefore, if the states can be induced to pay part of the cost. But the Social Security Act does not specify what proportion of the cost a state must carry in order to obtain the federal grant. It need pay only a nominal sum and leave the counties and cities to provide practically all of the pensions. If the states do this the average pensions will continue to be small.

To the aged person the conditions under which he can obtain assistance are almost as important as the amount of assistance he can get. In this respect the old-age pension is not a great deal better than the security given under the public welfare laws. It carries with it a strong tinge of charity and at least some of the stigma of the poor law.

In the first place the pensions are to be paid only to those who are needy. The Social Security Act does not say what is meant by needy people. Once again the decision will be left to each state. The existing state laws subject applicants for old-age pensions to many of the conditions applied to people seeking ordinary poor relief. States often refuse pensions to old people of whose morals or habits they disapprove. Drunkards or those who have failed without good reason to provide support for their wives or young children, as well as those who are tramps or beggars, are often deprived of the right to pensions.

Practically all states refuse pensions to people possessing incomes above a very low level. In all except two states, pensions are denied any aged person with relatives legally liable to support him and able to do so. Under the original Social Security Bill no account would have been taken of the income of relatives. Pensions would have been payable to an old person if his own income together with that of his spouse was inadequate. Since this clause was struck out of the Act, much of the burden of keeping the dependent aged will, in the future, as in the past, be borne by those who are young and still earning. Many of the aged will be compelled to continue living as unwanted guests in the homes

43

of relatives or children. The young will be compelled to support their parents as well as themselves and their children, and their chances of putting aside money to provide for an independent old age will be reduced.

The aroma of poor relief will hang over these pensions for a second reason. The aged are investigated in many states by the officials who are in charge of welfare relief. Not only do the ordinary public relief employees administer the pension law, but they do so in the poor law spirit. Some states even admit this close connection between old-age pensions and ordinary relief by calling their laws old-age "assistance," "aid," or "relief" rather than "pension" laws. The Social Security Act also uses the word "assistance" to describe this part of the program for helping the aged.

The Social Security Board will have some opportunity to remedy this state of affairs. The Act requires that states can obtain federal grants only if they "provide such methods of administration as are found by the Board to be necessary for the efficient operation of the plan." The Board may not dictate to the states what they must pay their employees or how they shall select them, but there seems no reason why it should not be able to insist that the investigation of the claims of the aged and the payment of pensions shall not be done by the poor relief administrators.

It will be easier to carry through such a change of policy if the Board has to deal only with one responsible authority in the state instead of hundreds. Each state desiring a federal grant must establish a single state agency to administer the pension law. This agency must furnish reports to the Social Security Board on request. In 1935, six of the states with pension laws still had no such supervising body. Unless there is a change in the spirit in which pension laws are administered it will be difficult to convince the aged that there is any advantage in calling the money they receive a pension rather than relief, especially where (as happened in seven states at the end of 1934) the average old-age pension is smaller than the average sum paid to old people as relief.

There is yet a third way in which the stigma of the poor law is likely, in spite of the Social Security Act, to remain attached to these old-age assistance pensions. The states are free, if they wish, to claim back from any estates left by pensioners who die the sums paid to them as pensions. Of the 30 states studied by the Committee on Economic Security, 23 recovered pensions from the grave in this way, and 21 retained the right to compel aged people to transfer their property to the pension authority before they would grant any pension. The federal government does not discourage this squeezing of the aged; it even insists on receiving a one-half share of the money thus obtained.

On the other hand, in order to mark off the pensions from ordinary relief the Act requires that any state obtaining help from the federal government shall allow any aged person the right of appeal if his request for a pension is refused. This appeal can be made to the central state agency in charge of pension administration which each state is required to set up. The fact that the Social Security Board will be generally supervising the state agencies will give aged people some protection against unfair treatment or political discrimination. The right of appeal itself suggests that a pension is a right rather than a grudging concession.

Who Can Obtain a Pension?

The number of people who will benefit by the old-age assistance plan will vary from state to state. If no pension laws are passed no old-age pensions will be paid. Even when states pass laws a great deal will depend upon the conditions they lay down. At the end of the 1935 legislative sessions only 39 states and the District of Columbia had pension plans of any kind. Aged de-

pendent people in 9 states will therefore obtain
no security under the Social Security Act, unless
their states pass the necessary laws. Whether
they will do so in order to take advantage of the
federal offer to share in the cost remains to be
seen. They probably will—but how soon? The
federal government has made it plain that the
states are to provide such security as is given to
those people who cannot be regarded as employ-
able. Hence in the future the states will have the
choice of paying relief to old people and financing
it entirely themselves, or paying pensions to
them and collecting half the cost from the federal
government. However much they may resent
the conditions laid down by the federal government they will probably find it worth their while
to meet them. The growing proportion of the
aged in our total population will every year
increase the pressure on them to pass the kinds
of laws suggested by the Social Security Act.

The mere passage of a state law is not enough.
At the beginning of 1935 there were three states
which had passed laws but had not put them
into effect. States have sometimes allowed the
counties to decide for themselves whether they
would grant the pensions provided for in the
state law. At the end of 1934 only 11 of the state
laws were state-wide in operation. In the remainder pensions were paid in only 64 per cent

of the counties of the states concerned. In the hope of making state pension laws a reality in every part of the country the Social Security Act provides that no federal grants will be paid unless the plan is in effect in all political subdivisions of the state, and if administered by them is mandatory upon them. The knowledge that this condition was likely to be included in the Security Act has already caused many states to change their laws. Yet at the end of 1935 there were still four states in which the payment of pensions was not mandatory on all counties.

Not all the needy aged persons living in states with pension laws will obtain security. The pensions are limited to certain kinds of people. All the states have an age limit. In the past this limit has been as high as seventy. In the hope of lowering this limit the federal grants under the Social Security Act will be paid only to those states which reduce the age limit to sixty-five. However, to give the states time to prepare themselves for the change, the limit may be as high as seventy until 1940. At the end of 1935, 27 states granted pensions at the age of sixty-five.

Many states have also restricted pensions to persons who have been American citizens for a considerable time. At the end of 1934, 21 states paid pensions only to people who had been

48

citizens for 15 years. Here too the federal government makes its offer to share in the cost conditional upon more generous state requirements. The states may continue to limit pensions to citizens of the United States, but they may not refuse them to people because they have not been citizens for a certain number of years. Even after the many changes carried through during 1935 there were still 11 states which demanded 15 years of citizenship.

In order to protect themselves from an influx of old people for the sole purpose of obtaining a pension, most of the state laws have provided that in addition to all the other conditions, pensioners must have resided within the state for a specified period. Sometimes the period of residence has been very long. In order to bring about more uniformity and to make it easier for old people to get pensions, the federal government offers grants on condition that states modify these requirements. In future any aged person otherwise qualified, in the states obtaining federal aid, will be able to obtain a pension if he has resided there for five years out of the last nine and has lived there continuously for one year. Nineteen of the states at the end of 1935 had residence requirements which will have to be changed in order to obtain federal aid.

49

Who Pays for the Pensions?

The money for the old-age pensions will be provided by the federal government and by the states. If the states ever decide to pay pensions of more than $30 a month they must put up more than 50 per cent of the total cost. But we shall probably not be far from the truth if we say that roughly one-half of the cost of this kind of old-age security will be provided by the federal government. As we shall see in Chapter Nine, it may obtain the money for this purpose from a number of sources. It may even, for the time being, use some of the money raised by the taxes on employers and workers levied under the Security Act. Until we know from what source the money comes we can say little about who finally pays the federal government's share of old-age assistance.

The remaining 50 per cent must be provided by the state and local authorities. The federal government requires that the states shall share in the costs, but it does not say how much that share shall be. The states may, therefore, continue to require the counties and the cities to contribute. The different states are likely to adopt different policies. They are also left quite free to decide what kinds of taxes they will levy in order to raise the necessary money. The counties and the states have, as a rule, provided the funds for this purpose out of general taxation. But they have occasionally tried to raise the money by imposing special taxes, the income from which has been earmarked to pay old-age pensions.

The answer to the question, "Who pays for old-age pensions?" will, therefore, depend upon the kinds of taxes that each state decides to collect. If the pensions are financed out of the general state or county funds, we can only say that all the taxpayers will contribute in the same proportion as they contribute to all the other kinds of state expenditure. But if the states decide to follow the example of Nebraska or Iowa, and raise the funds for old-age pensions out of a poll tax which must be paid by every person regardless of his income, we can be fairly certain that the poorer sections of the community will have to pay a larger share of the cost than they would if the money were provided out of most other taxes. On the other hand, if they decide to follow the example of New Jersey and finance the pensions out of inheritance taxes, workers will probably pay a smaller proportion of the cost (since very few of them pay inheritance taxes) than they would if the pensions were financed from the general funds.

51

Thus it is impossible to say who pays for old-age pensions. The distribution will vary from state to state. But it is easy to see that the average worker will bear a smaller share of the cost of the old-age pensions than of the cost of the old-age annuities, which are to be financed entirely by payments from employers and workers. Since the federal government normally obtains a greater proportion of its income from graduated income and corporation taxes than do the states, the more the federal government contributes to the cost of old-age pensions, the less will be the burden on the small man.

Summary

The greater proportion of the aged population will have to seek security in the second form made possible by the Act, namely, from the state-administered old-age pensions paid to needy persons. These people comprise, in addition to those gainful workers employed in agriculture, domestic service and independent employments, all the non-gainfully employed adults, many of whom are, like housewives, doing useful work but not for wages. To these will be added, for many years to come, the people whoseannuities under the first plan are too small to maintain them. All these people will obtain security only if their states pass the necessary laws.

The security they can hope for will be more pleasant than that given by the annuity plan in that they will not have had to pay special taxes all their working lives in order to get it. It will be financed out of general taxation of which they will have paid as a rule only a small part. But it will be much more unpleasant in that it will be available to them only if they are in need and have no relatives capable of supporting them. It will be paid to them as a concession and not as a right and will still carry quite a little of the stigma of poor relief. Unless the states change their policies, the average old-age pension will be very small. As a result, in the future as in the past, many thousands of young people will be called upon to support aged dependent relatives.

Chapter Four

THE UNEMPLOYED

No unemployed worker will receive any payment from the federal government under the Social Security Act. How then will the Act help the unemployed? They will benefit only if the federal government succeeds in its efforts to encourage states to give workers security against unemployment.

The security is to take the form of unemployment compensation. Workers will be given a right to cash benefits when they are unemployed regardless of their means, provided they have been employed for a certain period in the past. The money to pay for these benefits will be obtained mainly from a tax on employers. Very little of this kind of security would be provided if the matter were left entirely in the hands of the states. Since employers in each state compete against those in all the others, those in a state providing unemployment compensation would have a real grievance. They would be placed at a disadvantage compared with competitors in other states who are not taxed in this way.

The Social Security Act is designed to remove this obstacle in the way of states anxious to provide unemployment compensation and to finance it in this way. The device used is a 3 per cent tax on payrolls. This tax must be paid by all employers in the United States covered by the Act. If a state sets up an unemployment compensation plan and collects the funds by taxing payrolls the employers in that state may deduct what they pay to the state from the money they would otherwise have to pay the federal government. But they cannot escape the whole of the federal tax in this way. The Act permits them to balance what they paid the state against what they owe the federal government only up to 90 per cent of the federal tax. Thus, however much they pay to the state, they will always pay to the federal government $\frac{3}{10}$ of 1 per cent (*i.e.*, 10 per cent of the original 3 per cent federal tax).

As a result of this tax device it will not make much difference financially to employers whether their states provide unemployment compensation or not. For example, an employer with a payroll of $100,000 a year will be liable to pay to the federal government a tax of $3,000 a year. If his state sets up an unemployment compensa-

tion fund and collects from him a tax equal to
2.7 per cent of payroll, he will still only pay a
total annual tax of $3,000. Since 2.7 per cent is
90 per cent of 3 per cent, he will be entitled to
offset the whole of his state tax against what he
owes the federal government. Thus when he
makes out his federal tax return it will look like
this:

Tax due at 3 per cent on $100,000............. $3,000
Tax paid to state at 2.7 per cent of $100,000..... 2,700

    Net tax due federal government 0.03 per cent
      of $100,000............................ $ 300

He will pay $3,000 whether or not his state
provides unemployment compensation. If it
does, he divides his payment between the federal
government and his own state. If it does not, he
pays the entire sum to the federal government.
At worst he will have the added trouble of
making two tax returns.

Since he can escape only 90 per cent of the
federal tax however much he pays to his state
fund, an employer will still be at a disadvantage
as compared with competitors in other states if
his own taxes him at a higher rate than 2.7 per
cent of payroll. New York State, for instance,
will require employers after 1938 to pay to the
state 3 per cent of their payrolls. A New York

employer with an annual payroll of $100,000 will, as we have seen, owe the federal government $3,000. But although he will be contributing $3,000 to New York State, he will be excused only 90 per cent of what he owes the federal government. Thus in the end he will pay in taxes:

State Unemployment Compensation Plan....... $3,000
Federal Social Security Act Tax.............. 300
   (*i.e.*, total federal tax of $3,000 minus 90 per
    cent or $2,700)

      Net tax................................ $3,300

He will, in other words, be $300 a year worse off than his competitors who pay the federal 3 per cent tax (because their state has no unemployment plan) and who carry, on the same payroll, a tax of only $3,000.

Some states have attempted to persuade employers to stabilize employment by allowing those with an employment record better than average to pay a smaller payroll tax than the others. Unless some special arrangements were made in the Social Security Act for such plans, these employers would in future obtain no reward for their more regular operation. Although their states would collect a smaller tax from them, when they came to pay the federal tax they would have a correspondingly smaller sum to deduct from it. Thus the only difference would be that the more regular employers would pay a larger proportion of their 3 per cent tax to the federal government, and the irregular ones would pay a larger proportion to the state.

To make it possible for the states to adopt such plans, the Security Act provides what are known as Additional Credits. If an employer is paying less than the maximum state tax solely because he has satisfied the standards of regular employment set out in his state plan, he may deduct the full maximum state tax from his federal tax. In other words, in addition to deducting from his federal tax the money he actually pays to the state, he can also deduct the difference between this sum and what he would have to pay if he were taxed at the full rate levied on other employers by the state law. For example, an employer with a payroll of $100,000 operates in a state levying a maximum payroll tax of 2.7 per cent. But owing to his excellent employment record the state permits him to pay a reduced tax of 1 per cent of payroll. Under the state law he will pay $1,000 a year. Thanks to the Additional Credit allowed in the Social Security Act, he will pay to the federal government only $300, as can be seen from the following calculation:

Tax due federal government (3 per cent on $100,-
000)...................................... $3,000
Deduction for state tax
    Actual tax paid.................... $1,000
    Additional credit (*i.e.*, full state tax of
        $2,700 minus $1,000 actually paid)   1,700
                                            _____
                                             2,700
                                            _____
                                            $ 300

Thus the net tax paid by this man will be only
$1,300. As compared with other employers in
his state who will be paying the full tax of $3,000
he will be $1,700 better off. This is his reward for
stabilizing employment.

The unemployment compensation part of
the Social Security Act thus makes it possible
for every state to set up an unemployment
compensation plan financed by a payroll tax
up to 2.7 per cent without placing its industries
at a disadvantage as compared with those in
other states. For the next two years, however,
the payroll taxes the states can collect without
placing their employers at a disadvantage will
be somewhat less than this, for the full federal
3 per cent tax is not levied until 1938. It is only
1 per cent during 1936 and 2 per cent during
1937. In other words, unless the states are
willing to risk this financial disadvantage for
their industries, the federal act practically forces

them also to levy a 1 per cent and 2 per cent tax to begin with.

In addition to making state action possible, the Security Act offers a positive inducement to the states to pass unemployment compensation laws. A sum of money amounting in future years to $49,000,000 is set aside to pay the costs of administration of state plans. This money will be divided among the states on the basis of the size of their population, the number of people covered by their unemployment compensation laws and their costs of proper administration.

What Kind of Security?

The essence of unemployment compensation as distinct from ordinary relief is that a worker who is genuinely unemployed is entitled for a certain number of weeks to a cash benefit regardless of his private means. He can claim it because he has been employed as a wage earner for a certain length of time prior to becoming unemployed. The question that every worker will ask concerning this part of the Security Act is, therefore, how much of this kind of compensation it will provide and for how long the benefits will be paid.

Unemployed workers will get nothing at all unless their state sets up a plan, for there is no federal system as there is for providing annuities to the aged. But even if all the states act there may be not one but 48 different kinds and degrees of security against unemployment. It might have been expected that in return for its assistance in making possible the setting up of state unemployment compensation plans, the federal government would have defined what it meant by unemployment compensation. It might, for example, have stated that employers would be allowed to deduct their state payments from the federal payroll tax only if the state plan provided a certain minimum protection to unemployed workers. But curiously enough the Social Security Act has nothing to say on this vital point and the states are left entirely free to decide how much money shall be given, for how many weeks it shall be available, how long people must work to qualify for it, and how long they must wait before obtaining it after they become unemployed.

It is true that to obtain federal approval for its plan each state must deposit the money it collects for unemployment compensation in the Unemployment Trust Fund which is to be administered by the Secretary of the United States Treasury. This requirement may remove from the states the temptation to appropriate unemployment compensation funds for other purposes. The money collected will thus be available for the payment of benefits when needed. There may also be some saving of costs (and therefore more money for benefits) if the investment of the funds is handled by one instead of 48 authorities. But the terms on which these carefully protected and economically administered funds are to be distributed to unemployed workers are left to the discretion of the states.

The nearest the Security Act comes to saying how much security shall be given is to require that all the money collected by the states shall be used for the payment of unemployment compensation. This will prevent the states from using the money to pay the salaries of a large and costly body of bureaucrats. But the Act does not say within what period the money is to be spent on benefits. Far from stating that benefits *must* begin after a certain period of time, the Act does exactly the opposite and requires that *no* benefits shall be paid for the first two years after any state plan comes into effect. The object of this provision is to compel the state funds to build up a reserve. Nor does the federal law specify the amount or duration of the benefits or how long each worker must wait to receive his benefits after his state has begun to make payments. A state might, if it wished, save up the money year by year to pay benefits during the next ice age.

We can obtain some idea of the kind of security that workers are likely to obtain by observing what is already provided in the states which have set up unemployment compensation laws. The amount and duration of the benefits vary from one state plan to another. As a rule workers will be entitled to benefits equal to 50 per cent of their previous average weekly wages. In Wisconsin, however, benefits will be paid at this level only under certain conditions. In the District of Columbia they will obtain only 40 per cent but can claim additional benefits for a wife and children. In most states weekly benefits can never exceed a certain maximum, however high wages have been in the past. The usual limit is $15, although it is as high as $18 in Utah. All the existing plans except that of the District of Columbia and Washington provide also a minimum benefit. This minimum is usually about $5 a week, although it rises to $7 in California.

The length of time for which benefits will be paid differs from state to state. As a rule benefits are related to previous employment. For each so many days or weeks of previous employment a worker is entitled to a week's unemployment benefit. California, for example, provides that workers can claim one week of benefit for each previous four weeks of employment in a trade covered by the Act. In New York workers can obtain one week's benefit for each 15 days of insurable employment in the last year. But all states pay benefits only for a certain number of weeks in any year, however regularly a man had been employed in the past. As a rule this limit is 15 or 16 weeks in any one year, although in Wisconsin it is as low as 13. Some states extend the period for workers with an exceptionally good past employment record.

In all unemployment compensation plans it is usual to pay unemployment benefits only after workers have been unemployed for a certain length of time. This period varies from two weeks in Utah to six weeks in Washington. The most usual period is three weeks.

To obtain unemployment compensation benefits of any kind workers must have been engaged in occupations covered by the compensation acts for at least a certain period of time. Workers can most easily qualify in New Hampshire, where they must work only 60 days in such employments in the year preceding their application for benefits. It will be most difficult for them in Utah, where they will not be entitled to claim benefits at all unless they have worked for 20 weeks during the last 52.

How far will other states follow this general pattern? A great deal will depend on whether they set up plans solely in order to prevent the federal government from obtaining all the proceeds of the payroll tax or to help their employers to get Additional Credits. But if we suppose that a state is anxious to give as much protection to its unemployed workers as possible, the security that any worker can hope for will still be limited by the amount of money his state has to spend and the severity of unemployment there.

The size of the funds available to the states depends mainly upon the kinds of taxes that are levied. A state may impose taxes on employers or workers, or it may contribute funds from the proceeds of general taxation. In addition, if its law meets the conditions laid down in the Security Act it can obtain a federal grant to cover the costs of administration. While there is nothing in the Security Act to prevent a state from collecting contributions from workers, only five of the ten plans in existence at the end of 1935 have actually done so. Three of these plans require that workers shall not pay more than 50 per cent of what the employer pays. Collections from workers will not form a large part of the funds available for unemployment compensation. Provision for a contribution from the general tax fund exists only in the District of Columbia scheme, although in some states small sums are granted to cover the costs of administration.

The largest and most important source of income in the existing plans is, therefore, the tax on employers, and it is probable that this will be the case in any subsequent plans. How much then is likely to be raised from employers? In New York, Utah, and the District of Columbia the rate is 3 per cent but elsewhere the tax is only 2.7 per cent, or it is expressly stated in the law that no employer shall be asked to pay more than he is allowed to credit against the federal tax. It is unlikely that in future many states will collect more than 2.7 per cent from employers. For, as we have seen, they will place their employers at a competitive disadvantage if they do so. It is therefore important to know how much unemployment compensation can be financed by a payroll tax of 2.7 per cent or at most 3 per cent.

The Committee on Economic Security estimated that a 3 per cent payroll tax would yield enough money to pay each unemployed worker a benefit equal to 50 per cent of wages for between 10 and 15 weeks. The Committee based these estimates on calculations of past unemployment. They arrived at the 15-week period when they

considered unemployment in the years 1922–
1930. When the years of heavy unemployment
between 1930 and 1933 were also taken into
account, the benefits that could be financed
out of a 3 per cent tax fell to 10 weeks. If we
believe that we are unlikely ever again to experience such a depression, we are justified in saying
that a 3 per cent tax will enable us to pay benefits
to workers for as much as 15 weeks. If, however,
we believe that we have entered a new era
in which heavy unemployment will be much
more common, then we must accept the lower
estimate.

The Social Security Board adopts a middle
path and suggests that a 3 per cent tax on payrolls will permit at most the payment to unemployed workers of benefits equal to 50 per cent
of wages for 12 weeks after a waiting period of
four weeks. If the states confine themselves to a
2.7 per cent payroll tax they will, of course, be
able to offer slightly less security than this.

But benefits for 12 weeks could be paid only
if every unemployed worker had to wait four
weeks before receiving his first compensation
payment. If the waiting time were reduced to
three weeks, benefits could be paid out of a
3 per cent tax only for 11 weeks. A reduction of
the waiting period to two weeks would cut the
duration of benefit to 10 weeks.

The fact that the full 3 per cent federal payroll tax is payable only from the beginning of 1938 will probably not reduce the benefits a state can offer. For although in 1936 it is only 1 per cent and in 1937 only 2 per cent, the money raised in these years is to be used to build up a reserve. No benefits are payable until two years after a plan has been set up.

The estimates of the amount and duration of benefit that could be provided by a 3 per cent tax are, however, estimates for the country as a whole. But unemployment varies greatly from one state to another, some states having on the average almost twice as much unemployment as others. The benefits which can be paid from a 2.7 per cent or 3 per cent payroll tax will therefore vary from state to state. They will depend on the extent of unemployment and the view taken by each state as to how much money it must hold back to meet future unemployment.

In any case, these figures tell us only the maximum amount that a state *could* pay if it collected the full 2.7 per cent or 3 per cent tax from employers. Within this limit the actual security that any worker will get will depend upon the kind of unemployment compensation plan selected by his state. There are at least five plans which the states might adopt under the Social Security Act. These plans are the

68

pooled reserve, the individual plant reserve, the merit rating, and the guaranteed employment plans, or any combination of these four.

Under the simple pooled reserve system all employers pay the same percentage tax on payrolls. They continue to pay this tax through fat years and lean. The money obtained, together with whatever may be contributed by workers or by the state, is placed in a central pool out of which benefits are paid. The individual plant reserve plan provides for the taxes paid by each employer to be kept in a separate account or reserve. Once an employer has accumulated a reserve of a certain level, he is permitted to pay lower taxes or even no tax at all. Whenever his reserve falls below the limit prescribed in the law, he must again begin to pay taxes. The third method, known as merit rating, is a compromise between the first two. All the money collected is paid into a single central pool, but the taxes paid by employers will not be uniform. Those with a bad employment record will pay a larger tax, while those with a good record will pay a smaller tax on payrolls. The fourth method is the so-called guaranteed employment plan. Employers guarantee at least a certain number of weeks of work (40 under the Security Act) and pay taxes to build up a reserve to enable them to meet this guarantee. When they have accumulated a sum which the law regards as adequate they cease paying taxes. Finally a state may set up some combination of these plans. It might, for example, select the individual plant reserve method but require that even if an employer's reserve reaches the minimum level he must still pay a certain percentage of his payroll to a central pool.

Each of these plans gives a different measure of protection to the unemployed worker. It is important, therefore, to know how much security will be provided by each. Of all these methods the simple pooled reserve which is adopted, for example, in New York offers the greatest amount of protection to unemployed workers. The benefits paid to each worker depend not on the size of his own employer's reserve but on the amount of money in the state pool to which all employers contribute. Thus if the firm in which he worked is driven out of business by a more efficient rival, some part of the payroll taxes paid by the successful firm will be available to pay his unemployment benefits. In this way the full advantages of insurance are obtained. The money not needed by the more fortunate workers can be used to help the less fortunate. Also under this plan money can be collected from employers in good years and accumulated to help pay for unemployment in the bad years.

The plant reserve type of unemployment compensation, which is adopted in Wisconsin and Utah, operates very differently. If a man is out of work his benefits will be paid out of his own employer's reserve. If this is exhausted before he has received the full amount of benefit permitted under his state law he is out of luck. He has no claim on the unused reserve funds of other employers. Nor is it possible to accumulate money over many years so as to have larger funds to meet occasional heavy unemployment. For when his reserve reaches a certain sum, an employer does not have to pay any further taxes. In Wisconsin employers cease to pay the state tax when their reserve is more than 10 per cent of the annual payroll; in Utah they stop when they have a reserve equal to $100 per employee. Under the Social Security Act no state will be able to set up a reserve plan that calls for a reserve of less than 7½ per cent of the annual payroll of the preceding year. According to the Act it must also amount to "not less than five times the largest amount of compensation paid from such account within any one of the three preceding calendar years," but whether this means total compensation to all workers or the largest amount to any one worker is not clear. Even under these conditions less money will be collected under the plant reserve plan to provide economic security. For this reason and because a worker's benefits depend upon the size of the reserve of his own employer, the amount of security offered by the plant reserve plan is much less than that which can be given under the simple pooled reserve system.

In between the two, from the point of view of the unemployed worker, stands the merit rating system. Such a plan has been adopted in Alabama, California, District of Columbia, Massachusetts, New Hampshire, Oregon, and Washington. It may also be adopted in New York after 1939. In these states all the money raised is paid into a central pool. But if after three years' experience it is found that some employers have a better employment record than others, they may be permitted to pay a lower tax. Sometimes efforts to stabilize on the part of conscientious employers do not reduce the *total* of unemployment. They merely concentrate irregularity on workers employed by less scrupulous concerns. Unless at the same time these employers with the relatively worse record have to pay a higher tax, the total amount of money paid into the pool will be less, and the benefits payable to unemployed workers will be correspondingly reduced. The worker is likely to receive as much security as under the simple pooled reserve, only if the law requires that the average tax must never be less than the usual 2.7 or 3 per cent. Only three states require that the average tax shall never fall below 3 per cent. In states having a merit rating plan, employers, however good their record, must pay at least some tax, usually 1 per cent of payroll, to the central pool. But in only six of the states is there even a suggestion that the taxes will be increased for the employers with a bad record, and this for a very good reason. If the average tax is to be 2.7 or 3 per cent, employers whose rates are increased above this level will lose the protection from interstate competition afforded by the federal 3 per cent tax. Most states will be unwilling to penalize their employers in this way. Thus a merit rating system is likely to give workers less security than the simple pooled reserve, although they will obtain more than under the individual plant reserve.

We have so far considered these plans from the point of view only of the unemployed workers. It may be that the individual plant reserve and the merit rating plans will, in the end, give even more security. Although providing less unemployment benefit they may increase a worker's chances of obtaining a job. They have indeed been adopted in the hope of bringing about this result. Those who favor the individual plant reserve plan believe that if each employer is responsible for his own unemployed, he will make efforts to stabilize employment in order to save himself money. He can escape paying taxes only if his reserve is above the minimum required in the law. It will remain at this level only if he does not have to draw on it to pay unemployment benefits. He will therefore try to hold on to his workers as long as possible. In the same way those who favor a merit rating system expect that the desire to produce a good employment record entitling them to a tax reduction will encourage employers to stabilize employment.

Opinions differ greatly as to how far unemployment will be reduced by these methods. The most serious kinds of unemployment are, after all, outside the control of any individual employer. No employer can protect himself against the consequences of a general depression however hard he may try. At most he can control minor fluctuations. Some ways of stabilizing production may be quite costly and may even counterbalance any gain through a reduction in his payroll tax. It is also doubtful whether if he has not tried to stabilize production until now a relatively small payroll tax will be a sharp enough spur to make him attempt it.

It is indeed unlikely that job security will be increased sufficiently to counterbalance the very real loss of unemployment protection that these methods involve. Workers under the merit rating plans will, however, obtain more security than those under plant reserve systems. They have about the same chance of benefiting from the efforts of employers to regularize employment, plus the opportunity to obtain unemployment benefits out of a central pool if their employers are unsuccessful. Under a plant reserve plan if employment is not regularized, the amount of unemployment benefit depends entirely on the size of their own employer's reserve.

Guaranteed employment, the fourth kind of unemployment compensation permitted under the Social Security Act, has not yet been adopted by any state. Employers guarantee at least 40 weeks of employment (for 30 hours a week) and pay benefits to workers only if they are unable to fulfill this guarantee. Under the Social Security Act they must build up a reserve equal to at least 7½ per cent of the wages they would have to pay to make good this guarantee. If they have worked for 40 weeks, workers cannot claim any further benefits even though they are out of a job for the other 12 weeks of the year. They are, however, assured of at least 40 weeks of full wages every year. Twelve weeks of uncompensated unemployment each year can scarcely be called economic security. Yet economic life is now so insecure that many workers would regard such a guarantee as superior to the other kinds of unemployment compensation. But it is doubtful whether many employers will be willing or able to guarantee even 40 weeks of work to their employees in the present uncertainty of business prospects.

The protection afforded workers by any combination of these plans varies with the kinds of plan selected. If a state adopted the plant reserve method but required employers to pay at least some tax to a central pool, however high their reserve, the steady employer would be rewarded, although to a less extent than before. But workers whose employers closed down before an adequate reserve had been built up would at least obtain some assistance from the central pool. Similarly, if employers in a guaranteed employment plan were compelled to pay at least a certain percentage of payroll to a central fund, even though they had accumulated the required 7½ per cent reserve, the workers would benefit. They would be able to obtain some compensation if they happened to become unemployed after receiving their guaranteed 40 weeks of work. The steady employer would not receive so great a reward for his efforts but he would still be better off than other employers who paid the full maximum rate with no deductions at all. The original Security Bill had provided that employers could obtain the Additional Credit only if they contributed at least 1 per cent of payroll to a central pool, however good their record or high their reserve. But this clause which would have increased the security of workers was dropped as the bill passed through Congress.

The nature of the security given by an unemployment compensation scheme depends not only on the amount and duration of the cash benefit but also on the conditions under which it is paid. All unemployment compensation plans pay benefits only to people who are out of work through no fault of their own. One way of testing a worker's desire to obtain employment is to offer him a job and see if he refuses it. But as a rule workers are not penalized for refusing certain kinds of jobs. Even the federal government, which, as we have seen, has tried to give states as much freedom as possible in their unemployment compensation plans, felt it necessary to lay down standards in this matter. It will not recognize any state plan which denies benefits to people who refuse to accept work if a job is vacant only because of a strike, lockout or other labor dispute; if the wages, hours or other conditions are substantially less favorable than those prevailing for similar jobs in the locality, or if, in order to obtain the job, a worker must belong to a company union or promise not to belong to a trade union.

With these three exceptions, the states may offer unemployed people any kinds of jobs they wish, and deny them benefits if they refuse to accept them. There is nothing in the Act to prevent a state from offering an unemployed worker employment of quite a different nature from that to which he has been accustomed in the past. It can offer a skilled worker an unskilled job, so long as the rates of pay are the ordinary unskilled wages, and if he refuses it he may be denied benefit.

In the hope of securing methods of administration that protect the rights of workers and ensure that they are given the widest possible opportunities for finding a job, the Security Act requires that all the benefits must be paid through public employment offices in the state or other agencies approved by the Social Security Board. Unless benefits are paid in this way employers in the state concerned will be denied the privilege of deducting their state payroll tax from what they owe the federal government. In addition, before a state can obtain federal money to pay the costs of administration it must set up impartial tribunals to give a fair hearing to workers whose claims for benefit are refused. It must also make reports from time to time to the Social Security Board on matters on which the Board requires information. Finally it must cooperate with those departments of the United States government which deal with the unemployed, namely, the Public Works and Works Progress groups, supplying, when requested, information about the job history and duration of unexpired benefit rights of workers receiving unemployment compensation.

Who Can Obtain Unemployment Compensation?

Whether an unemployed person will obtain the elusive compensation made possible by the Act depends on where he works, at what trade he works, how long he has been unemployed, and when the state in which he works passed the unemployment compensation law.

Workers in states which pass no law will obtain no unemployment benefit. By the end of 1935 laws had been passed in nine states and the District of Columbia. The Social Security Act encourages the others to follow suit in two ways: it removes the fear of placing the employers in the state at a disadvantage in competing with those outside, and it offers states financial help in meeting the costs of administration. There is no way of prophesying how many states will respond to these inducements. The Act will undoubtedly assist state action where there is already a desire for it. Employers must pay the 3 per cent federal payroll tax whether the state acts or not. But if it sets up no plan none of the money thus collected will be spent within its own borders. Part of the money collected from its employers might be used to pay the costs of administering unemployment compensation plans set up by other states, which might be mortifying for the state providing the money.

On the other hand, employers may well feel that it is bad enough to have to pay a federal tax without the bother of also making returns to their own state and being investigated by two sets of officials. They may fear that when workers discover that they are entitled to unemployment benefits as a right they will continuously increase their demands, with the result that the state will be compelled to collect higher and higher payroll taxes. They may also fear that workers will refuse jobs at low wages if they know that they can obtain unemployment pay for at least a certain number of weeks. Thus employers may oppose the setting up of any plan.

In the same way the offer of the federal government to assist the states by paying a considerable part of the cost of administering

schemes will probably serve as a strong inducement to act only where there is already a movement in favor of unemployment compensation
which has been discouraged because of the
costs involved. It is unlikely that many states
will be deterred from setting up compensation
plans because they are unwilling to meet the
standards laid down in the Security Act. These
conditions are, as we have seen, surprisingly
few and mild. Constitutional amendments may,
however, be necessary in some states before all
the federal conditions can be fulfilled.

Whether states act or not will depend ultimately upon their estimate of the consequences
of doing nothing. If a state expects that in
future the federal government will do nothing
for its unemployed workers during the first
12 or 15 weeks of their unemployment, it will
probably set up a compensation plan. It can
thus finance the relief of its unemployed out
of money that would otherwise flow to the
federal government. But if it expects that
the federal government will take care of the
unemployed anyway, it may decide not to take
the trouble to set up a compensation plan.
The action taken by the states under the
Security Act will depend in part, therefore, upon
the anticipated relief policy of the federal
government.

81

Even if all 48 states pass unemployment compensation laws, there will be many unemployed workers not entitled to benefits. The federal government imposes the payroll tax only upon certain groups of employers. These groups are almost but not quite the same as those paying the payroll taxes for old-age annuities. The annuity tax is paid by employers in respect of all workers but only up to the first $3,000 of the wages or salary paid. The unemployment compensation tax makes no distinction, and employers must pay a tax based upon the full salary of the workers who are covered. Employers of casual workers will pay the tax and such workers may, therefore, be entitled to unemployment compensation although not to old-age annuities. On the other hand, the unemployment compensation tax excludes two groups who are covered by the old-age annuities plan: those employed by relatives and those working for small employers. The first group is probably not very important, but the exclusion of the latter seriously limits the protection given by the Security Act. Unless employers have a labor force of at least eight workers for at least 20 weeks in a year they will pay no payroll tax. In consequence, about 5,000,000 people may be deprived of the advantages of unemployment compensation. This exclusion of the employees of small concerns has a number of other serious disadvantages which will be discussed in Chapter Eight.

In addition to these two groups of people the unemployment compensation part of the Social Security Act excludes workers in agriculture, domestic service in a private home, shipping, the United States government and state services, and all of the non-profit-making organizations excluded from the old-age annuities plan.

The Security Act does not forbid the states to provide compensation to people in employments exempt from the federal payroll taxes. States are very unlikely, however, to be so open-handed because employers in these trades who pay state taxes would not be protected from the competition of employers in other states who do not pay such taxes. Some of the employments excluded from the federal tax are not subject to interstate competition. It would be quite possible for a state to include domestic servants, its own state employees, and members of non-profit-making organizations in its unemployment compensation plan, since these groups do not compete with employers in other states. A number of the states have already passed laws which include workers whose employers have less than eight but more than four employees. And in this way their laws are more generous than the Federal Security Act. But since most of these laws were passed at a time when it was expected that the federal law would also cover employers of four or more workers, it is probable that in the future many states will change their laws so that they cover the same employers who are affected by the federal payroll tax. In general, therefore, only workers employed in trades subject to the federal payroll tax are likely to receive compensation. Benefits will be limited, in the main, to the employees of the medium and large sized industrial and commercial concerns.

Migratory workers will have difficulty in obtaining benefits even if they work for a time in states with unemployment compensation laws. If they become unemployed when in a state that has no law they will receive benefits only if special arrangements have been made by the original state to pay benefits wherever its workers may be. The difficulty of arranging for these payments will often mean that migratory workers will get nothing. Even a worker who has had jobs in two states, both providing unemployment compensation, may lose his rights. His period of work in each state may be too short to permit him to claim benefits, although when added together they would amount to the minimum period required by the laws of either state. Such a worker will have a right to benefits only if the two states agree to count employment in the other as if it were performed within its own borders. Workers can be fully protected in this way only if each state makes an agreement with each of the 47 other states.

The third condition affecting a man's chances of obtaining benefit is the length of time for which he is unemployed. Since none of the state laws pays benefits indefinitely, workers who are unemployed for longer than the 12 or 15 weeks provided for in the laws must seek some other kind of security. Similarly, as benefits are normally payable only to those who have worked in the specified employments for a certain period in the past, none of the people who are now unemployed will obtain any protection. They will earn the right to benefit only if they again find a job and hold it or other jobs for the required length of time.

Finally, the federal law permits no approved state plan to pay benefits within two years after the scheme is set up. The employees in the 39 states which had not passed unemployment compensation laws by 1936 cannot, therefore, obtain any security until 1938. Employees in states whose legislatures delay action after 1936 must wait even longer.

The result of all these exclusions and limitations is that even if all states pass unemployment compensation laws relatively few workers can obtain benefits. The Social Security Board estimated that only 22.3 million workers or about 46 per cent of the total gainfully employed population would have been covered in 1930. By 1933 increased unemployment had reduced this number to 14.6 million.

Who Pays for Unemployment Compensation?

The money to provide unemployment compensation may be drawn from three sources: from taxes on employers, taxes on workers, and the general tax funds of a state. We have already seen that the greater part of the money is likely to be raised by taxes on employers, and (unless the states are prepared to penalize their smaller employers) only from employers of eight or more workers. In the expectation that the federal law would have covered employers of four or more workers many states lowered their limit to this level. But unless the federal law is amended in the near future they will probably relieve employers of four to seven workers from the necessity of contributing.

Even the 49 million dollars provided by the federal government to pay the costs of state administration will come from the same source. The necessary money will be yielded by the 10 per cent of the payroll tax that is retained by the federal government, whatever action the states may take.

Unless the states change their financing methods, relatively little of the money to finance unemployment compensation benefits will be supplied by contributions from workers or from general taxation. Five states provide for contributions from workers but as a rule such contributions are not to exceed one-half of what the employer pays. Funds have been granted out of general taxation to meet costs of administration in five states, but only the District of Columbia makes an appropriation toward benefits.

Summary

The unemployment compensation program of the Social Security Act is thus far from simple. To make it possible for states to set up plans financed by a 2.7 per cent payroll tax on employers the federal government goes to a great deal of trouble. It imposes a 3 per cent payroll tax on employers of a certain number of workers to persuade states to set up unemployment compensation plans and so get the money back within their own borders when their workers are unemployed. Although permitting employers to offset contributions to the state compensation fund against the federal tax due, it retains always 10 per cent of the tax (or 0.3 per cent of payrolls) which it uses to assist the states in the administration of their plans.

Yet after going through these elaborate motions to make it easy for the states to set up something called "unemployment compensation," the Security Act fails to specify on just those points which matter most to the unemployed what that compensation is to be. It lays down no standards concerning the minimum amount and duration of benefit, the length of employment necessary to quality for it, or the waiting period that must elapse after unemployment begins before benefits are payable.

As a result, it is impossible to say what kind of security will result from this part of the Act. Much will depend upon the amount of money the states decide to raise, the severity of unemployment in the different states and the type of compensation plan they adopt. The scope of the plans is equally unforecastable. Workers will get no protection if their states pass no laws, even if their employers pay the 3 per cent federal payroll tax. If laws are passed they are likely to cover only those affected by the federal tax. Compensation will thus be confined in the main to the employees of the middle-sized and larger industrial and commercial concerns. Most of the money is likely to be provided by taxes on employers. Workers are likely to feel that the mountainous labors of the Committee on Economic Security and of Congress have produced a disappointingly small mouse.

Chapter Five

THE SICK AND DISABLED

How can society be protected from the hazards of ill health? The obvious answer is, of course, that illness should be prevented. Many of the most costly diseases could be prevented if we devoted more time and money to the study of their causes and the methods of eradicating them. A number of the more spectacular diseases have been almost stamped out in this way. But we have still far to go. Prevention is a slow process. Until we can completely prevent sickness there will remain the problems of providing treatment for the sick and income for those who are too ill to earn.

The Prevention of Sickness

The Social Security Act encourages preventive work by authorizing the federal government to spend 10 million dollars a year on public health work. Of this sum 2 million dollars will be spent by the United States Public Health Service. This department of the federal government has for many years been investigating public health problems which are of a national character. Various parts of the country are affected by diseases about which little is known and the control of which demands federal action. Sometimes the cost of studying them is beyond the means of the state or states most seriously affected. Sometimes they are best studied by comparing the course of the disease in different parts of the country. And this is often difficult for any single state to do. Sometimes action by one state to improve its public health menaces the health of other states. For example, if cities located near the source of rivers use these rivers for the disposal of their sewage, others lower down the stream may suffer. The federal government alone can take the initiative and convince the various authorities of their common interest in so important a matter.

The United States Public Health Service, which has carried on work of this kind in the past, has always been limited by lack of money. The 2 million dollars granted for this work under the Security Act will make possible preventive work previously out of the question. Yet all those who are familiar with the work of the health service believe that this sum is far from adequate to finance all the work that needs to be done.

The remaining 8 million dollars granted for preventive health work is to be distributed among the states to help them improve their local public health service. There is ample room for improvement in many parts of the country. Of the 3,000 counties in the United States, only 528 have full time health supervision, and of these only 21 per cent had a staff and were providing a service that was regarded as adequate in 1933. During the depression cities have steadily reduced their expenditure on public health in spite of the greatly increased need for health services. One of the reasons for this decline in expenditure is, of course, the fact that health services were financed out of local taxes. With falling income and increased demands for unemployment relief, many of the cities economized on health work. The offer of assistance from the federal government is therefore of the first importance.

The 8 million dollars will be distributed among the various states so as to help those which are most in need. The Surgeon General of the Public Health Service (who is in charge of the distribution of the funds) has been instructed to divide the money among the various states on the basis of their population, their special health problems, and their financial needs. But before doing so he has to consult with the local health authorities, and the various states and territories must submit plans showing how they would spend the money.

The Treatment of Sickness

The Social Security Act also touches the second of the problems presented by ill health: namely, the provision of medical assistance to the sick. This assistance is to be given, however, only to young children and mothers.

The federal government is embarking on no new policy in encouraging the states to spend money on the health of mothers and children. Between 1922 and 1929 it granted money under the Sheppard-Towner Act for this very purpose. These federal funds were withdrawn in 1929, and many of the states abandoned their programs. Twenty-three states now have no special funds for maternal or child health, or spend less than $10,000 a year for these purposes. Yet the need for maternal and child health service is undeniable. The most dangerous year of life is the first. Although the number of children dying in this dangerous period has been steadily falling for many years, the death rate is still far too high. The health of children is greatly improved where there are clinics to which mothers can bring their sickly children and where they themselves obtain treatment and advice.

Accordingly, the Social Security Act provides $3,800,000 to be paid to the states to help them to develop public health, nursing, and child health treatment, and a further $200,000 to meet the administrative expenses of the federal government in carrying through such a program. The states will obtain federal aid only if they develop approved health services. Most of the money will be divided among the states roughly in proportion to the number of children born in each. At most the federal government will pay one-half of what the state spends. But to assist those parts of the country where there is especial need for child health services, $980,000 of the total of $3,800,000 is to be distributed according to the financial needs of the states on a non-matching basis, special attention being paid to the needs of the rural areas and those suffering from severe economic distress.

The states (as when seeking federal aid in providing old-age assistance), in order to obtain grants, must satisfy conditions laid down by the federal government. A state must share in the costs and not require the counties and cities to provide all the funds. It must set up a special state health agency to supervise the program, and its methods of administration must be approved by the federal authority (in this case the Chief of the Children's Bureau). It must report from time to time to the federal government. Last but not least, it must improve and extend local maternal and child health services by local child health groups, it must arrange for cooperation between these groups and the medical, nursing, and welfare organizations, and it must set up demonstration services in needy areas or among especially needy groups. If the state plan meets these conditions, then, within the limits of the total sum granted by the Act, the federal government will share part of the total sum expended on maternal and child health services.

The Security Act provides health service to children in yet another way. It permits the federal government to spend every year $3,000,000 to care for crippled children. Once again the government confines itself to helping the states to give better service by offering grants on terms intended to raise the standards prevailing in the states. Of this money, $150,000 will be used to cover the federal costs of administration. Each state will get $20,000 plus a share in the remaining $1,830,000 determined by its need and the cost of such services. But instead of using the total number of live births in each state as the basis of distribution, the federal agency (again, the Children's Bureau) will use the number of crippled children in each.

A number of conditions must be met by a state before it obtains these grants. The state must itself contribute money. It must establish a spe-

94

cial agency to administer the program, and its methods of administration must be satisfactory to the Chief of the Children's Bureau. It must pay special attention to the needs of the rural areas and those suffering especially from economic depression. It must develop methods for seeking out crippled children and must provide them with medical, surgical, corrective and other services and hospital treatment where necessary. In order to ensure the smoothest possible operation of these plans the state must secure the cooperation of the local medical, health, nursing, and welfare groups and other agencies which have been helping physically handicapped children to take up suitable work.

Income during Sickness or Disability

Two groups of people whose earning power is diminished because of physical disability are provided for in the Social Security Act. The federal government endeavors to assist blind people to obtain pensions and to increase the earning power of the physically handicapped by giving them guidance and training.

Pensions for the Blind

More than half the states have provided pensions for needy blind people in the past. Under the Security Act the federal government will not itself pay such pensions but it will assist the states to do so. It offers to pay one-half the cost of pensions to blind people who are in need, plus 5 per cent of its share to cover costs of administration. It will not share in the cost of any pension over $30 a month. In spite of this limit to the amount of federal aid, the offer to share expenses will undoubtedly increase the security of blind people in the future.

State pensions have generally been small. During 1934 they averaged $20.01 per person per month and ranged from 83 cents in Arkansas to $33.12 in California. All states with the exception of California will have to increase their pensions to take full advantage of the federal offer of $15 a month per person. Twelve of them will have to raise the maximum written into their laws.

The Act sets no minimum pensions, and, as in the case of the old-age pensions, the states may, if they wish, use the federal grants, not to improve the security of the blind but to save themselves money. A state can, however, obtain a federal grant only if it pays some of the costs of the pensions. In 1935, 15 of the states contributed nothing. Many counties have been compelled to discontinue or reduce benefits because of financial weakness. The enforced participation of the states with their greater financial resources may make possible more generous pensions. But the absence of any specification of the proportion of the cost to be paid by a state (as distinct from its political subdivisions) means that the states may still thrust a large part of the burden on the counties, to the disadvantage of the pensioner.

The blind pension laws have, on the whole, carried less of the pauper taint than the old-age pension laws. All but two of the states limit pensions to blind persons of inadequate means, but they take a more generous view of need than in the case of aged people. Only 11 states refuse pensions to those having relatives able to support them. As a rule a blind person must prove merely that he has "means insufficient for self-support," and only slightly more than one-third of the state laws set a definite property or income limit. No pension may be paid under the Security Act to any blind person who is drawing an old-age pension.

To protect the rights of blind people claiming a pension, each state receiving federal assistance must give a fair hearing to those whose claims are refused. The Social Security Board may (as under the old-age pension plan) call for reports to ensure that the conditions laid down in the Act are complied with. Each state must set up a single state agency to be responsible for adminis-

tration if it wishes to obtain federal aid. In 1935
there were still 12 states in which the county was
the final authority.

Blind people will obtain pensions subsidized
by the federal government only if they live in
states which pass the necessary laws. By the
fall of 1935, 27 states had blind pension laws.
But again, like the old-age pension laws, they
were not enforced throughout each state. Some
counties, as we have seen, paid no pensions
because they had no funds. Two of the laws
merely empowered the state to pay pensions if it
so wished, while seven others left the counties
free to grant pensions or not. During 1934,
16 per cent of all the counties in states having
blind pension laws had not put a pension system
into force. To make pensions available to a
larger number of blind people, the Security Act
provides that before any state can obtain federal
assistance the state plan must be operative in all
the political subdivisions of the state. If the laws
are administered by local authorities they must
be mandatory upon them.

The states may (and five of them do) limit
pensions to blind people who are citizens. But
if they hope for federal aid they may not require
a pensioner to have been a citizen for any
specified length of time. They may, and usually
do, limit pensions to people who have been

living in their states for a certain number of years. But again it is a condition of federal aid that they shall not require any would-be pensioner to have lived in the state for more than five out of the last nine years, or to have lived there continuously for more than one year preceding his application. Many states will have to change their laws in this respect.

Most states limit the payment of pensions to persons in certain age groups. Even in states which have enacted blind pension laws, the security obtained by blind people will, therefore, depend to a large extent on the standards and conditions laid down in their own state.

The funds for blind pensions will be provided half by the federal government and half by the state (and local) authorities, so long as pensions do not exceed $30 a month. The federal government's share, together with the additional 5 per cent to cover the costs of administration, will be provided out of the general federal funds.

The states and counties have adopted a variety of methods of raising the money. As a rule they draw on the general tax funds, though special taxes on property or on liquor are occasionally used. The only state in which it can be asserted with certainty that the blind pay no part of the costs of their own security is Arkansas, where

99

the funds are raised by a tax on billiards and pool-rooms. The counties usually finance blind pensions out of the general county funds, although in five states they may levy a special tax on property.

Training and Guidance for the Handicapped

Physically handicapped persons obtain no direct increase of security under the Act. But indirectly they will probably benefit from additional money appropriated for vocational rehabilitation. Since 1920 the federal government and most of the states have cooperated in a program of economic reclamation for the physically handicapped. Those disabled in industry or suffering from physical incapacity for any reason have been given training, guidance, and general assistance in obtaining work suitable to their special needs and abilities. No money is spent on personal maintenance of disabled persons. They receive, however, individual treatment which may take the form of furnishing artificial limbs or appliances which will increase their earning capacity, or special training and guidance followed up by visits to the disabled worker if he has been placed in a new job.

Under the existing arrangement the federal government assists the states engaged in rehabilitation work. The funds are administered

by the Division of Educational Rehabilitation
in the Federal Office of Education. The available
money is used for matching expenditure by the
states. No state can obtain from the federal
government more money than it provides itself.
Three states still spend nothing. But however
much is spent in a state it can claim from the
federal government only a sum equal to its
proportionate share of the total federal grant
available. This proportion is determined by the
size of its population in relation to that of other
states.

As a result of this program many thousands
of people who would otherwise have been cut
off from the working life of the normal adult
have been enabled to obtain employment and
have become partially, if not wholly, self-
supporting. But the program has always been
limited by a shortage of funds. It has been
estimated that each year about 84,000 people are
disabled through accident and disease. Yet in
1934 when the service reached a peak, it was
possible to rehabilitate only 8,000 people. The
total number assisted in the whole period
between 1920 and 1935 was only 68,000.

The Social Security Act, by increasing the
funds at the disposal of the federal government,
will make possible a considerable extension of
the program. It increases the existing annual

grant of $1,000,000 by $863,000 for the year ending June, 1936, and by $2,140,000 a year thereafter. Of these sums $841,000 in the first year, and $1,938,000 in subsequent years, is to be used for grants to the states and to Hawaii. The remainder is to be used to cover the costs of administration of the federal government. The money will be provided out of the general funds at the disposal of the federal government. Since no special taxes are imposed to provide the money, the burden will be diffused among the population as a whole.

Why Not Health Insurance?

The principle of social insurance used in connection with old-age and unemployment compensation has not been used by the Social Security Act to provide security against the consequences of sickness. That 22 other countries have adopted health insurance schemes suggests that they are more than a social reformer's dream. The use of insurance to pool the risks of ill health is by no means an unfamiliar device. Voluntary sickness insurance plans already exist in a great many communities. Individuals in the middle income groups often contribute regularly, weekly, or monthly, in order that when they are sick they can obtain medical attention free, or at a reduced rate. Many people contribute toward hospital insurance funds so that when they are sick they can go to a hospital without having to pay the heavy bills that would otherwise fall due.

A compulsory health insurance system merely extends this way of providing against insecurity due to ill health to a wider circle of people. It is easy for healthy individuals to forget the cost of sickness. Many of those who most need protection will not secure it under a voluntary plan because their day-to-day necessities are so pressing that they are tempted to put no money aside against the chance that they may be sick and unable to earn in the future. Social health insurance is a way of forcing people to provide against the risk of sickness in order that the cost to each person may be reduced.

We have already adopted the compulsory insurance principle to secure income to workers whose earning power is reduced on account of industrial accidents. In 46 states employers must provide compensation for workers who are injured or killed while at work. In addition to cash payments to those who can no longer earn or whose earning power is impaired, employers are also liable, in all but 3 of these states, to provide for the medical and surgical care of injured workers. To make certain that an employer will be able to meet these claims, should accidents occur, all 44 states except Alabama had by 1934 required employers either to insure against their compensation risks or to give proof that they could meet claims likely to be made upon them. By compulsory insurance the rights of workers can thus be assured without imposing a ruinous burden on any individual employer.

Under a compulsory health insurance plan workers, and often employers, pay regular contributions in return for which workers obtain the right to various benefits. In many countries the state also contributes toward these benefits in recognition of the fact that those in the lower income groups do not have enough income to pay the full cost of adequate treatment even on an insurance basis. Health insurance benefits are usually of two kinds: on the one hand, workers (and often their entire families) obtain the right to the services of a doctor, and, as a rule, medicines either free or at a greatly reduced price. Some plans provide also for hospital and clinical treatment as well as dental services. On the other hand, when insured workers are so ill that they cannot continue to work, they obtain compensation for lost wages in the same way as unemployed workers obtain compensation under unemployment insurance or compensation plans.

In a health insurance system workers have the right to select the doctor by whom they wish to be treated from a list or panel of doctors who have agreed to cooperate with the insurance plan. Under some plans workers may change their doctor whenever they wish, in others they must give a certain amount of notice. The medical men in turn are free to cooperate or not. If a doctor is willing to treat insurance patients, he receives a fixed sum per year for each person selecting him. He may refuse individual patients if he wishes. To many doctors the assurance of a certain income per year from insurance patients is a great advantage, and any temptation to pocket the money and give them only perfunctory treatment is held in check by the knowledge that dissatisfied patients may change to another doctor. In the most successful plans the doctors work under the general supervision of committees or boards consisting of members of their own profession. These representatives of medical men arrange with the lay administrators as to how much of the available money is to be used for fees to individual doctors and how much for financing clinics and paying for the services of specialists.

Compensation for time lost on account of illness under a health insurance plan takes the form of cash benefits usually paid weekly. As a rule no benefits are paid for the first few days of sickness. The patient's condition is certified by the doctor in attendance and disputed cases are heard by medical referees.

Summary

What then are we to say about the attack made by the Social Security Act on the problem of insecurity due to ill health? Obviously it makes only a very small beginning. The money granted for prevention falls short of what is required and little is done to meet the needs of those people who are already sick. Only children and mothers will receive any direct treatment. Cash payments to those physically unable to work are limited to the blind, while the physically handicapped are given advice and training. But the ordinary man or woman prevented by sickness from working, or needing medical attention, gets no increased security. The problems of providing adequate medical attention at a cost that will not ruin the patient, and assuring some income to those who are too sick to earn, are largely unsolved. A social health insurance plan which would do much toward meeting both these needs has not been embodied in the Social Security Act.

Chapter Six

WIDOWS AND ORPHANS

THE Social Security Act does not do very much for all those whose customary bread-winners have died or deserted them. Two groups of such dependent people will, however, benefit directly or indirectly under the Act, namely, dependent children and widows, the provision for children being more adequate than that for widows.

Security for Dependent Children

The desirability of providing for dependent children other than by ordinary public welfare assistance has long been recognized. Children who have lost one or both parents, or whose main breadwinner can no longer provide for them, have in the past been assisted in two ways. They have been placed in orphanages or institutions, or they have been permitted to remain at home with their mothers or other relatives who are supplied out of public funds with an income to care for the children. The second is the more satisfactory method for both the child and the community in general.

Since 1911 an increasing number of states has recognized the advantage of this method of providing for dependent children, and so-called mothers' pension plans have been developed to supply the necessary income. The mothers or relatives who care for dependent children receive an income supposedly sufficient to make it unnecessary for them to work in order to obtain the necessities of life.

The Social Security Act offers "grants to states for aid to dependent children." The grant takes the form of a federal offer to share one-third of the cost of monthly pensions paid to relatives undertaking responsibility for bringing up needy children. In the past the sums granted have often been so inadequate that the mothers were compelled to seek employment to supplement their small pensions. During 1933 and 1934 the pensions have varied from $7.29 per month per family in Oklahoma to $60.14 in the District of Columbia. It is to be hoped that the states will use the federal subsidies to pay more generous pensions rather than to pay the same pensions as before and saddle the federal government with part of the cost. But there is no certainty that the federal grants will benefit needy children rather than state and county taxpayers.

The Act prescribes no minimum pension as a condition of federal aid. The Bill as it was first drafted required that the monthly pension must be adequate "to provide, when added to the income of the family, a reasonable subsistence compatible with decency and health." This condition disappeared from the Bill as it wormed its way through Congress, and there is now no limit to the smallness of the pension that may be paid by the states.

The federal government applies pressure to secure more adequate pensions by making its grants to the states conditional upon their carrying part of the burden. They may not pass the entire cost on to the counties and cities. At the end of 1934, out of the 45 pension plans, there were only 14 in which any part of the funds was provided by the state. The rest of the money was supplied from local funds, and state contributions throughout the country averaged rather less than one-sixth of the total sum spent. Where states helped to finance the pensions, they were usually higher than where the state had not assisted. The lowest pensions were found in states where all the money was supplied by the hard-pressed local authorities. The federal government hopes, by insisting that the states share the cost with their counties and cities, to induce the payment of more generous pensions. It does not, however, specify what proportion of the cost must be borne by the state.

The stimulus to the states to develop their pension laws will, in any case, be less than it was under the old-age pension plan, for the federal government does not offer them so much encouragement. It pays to the states only up to one-third of their expenditure and nothing at all for administration. It has set an upper limit to the individual pensions which it will help to finance. It will pay only up to $6 for one dependent child and only up to an additional $4 for each additional dependent child. If a state grants more generous pensions, it must pay out of state funds all the amount in excess of this sum.

The Security Act places few limitations on the conditions under which the pensions have to be paid. They are to be limited to needy dependent children but the Act nowhere defines the word "needy." The original Bill contained a definition but this too was struck out. These pensions do not, however, carry any liability upon the children to repay them when they grow up. Persons refused a pension have the right to appeal to the single agency which must be set up by each state to administer the plan. To ensure the proper methods of administration this agency must make reports from time to time to the Social Security Board.

The number of children obtaining increased security as a result of this part of the law will depend upon the number of states setting up state-wide pension plans, the age limit that they fix for the payment of pensions, and the conditions they impose as to residence.

At the present time three states (Alabama, Georgia, and South Carolina) still have no so-called mothers' pension laws. Despite the existence of laws in 45 states, only about 280,000 children received such aid at the end of 1934, although at the same time no less than 719,000 children were receiving aid from the Federal Emergency Relief Administration. Thus the state laws assist only about one-fourth of the children in need, and this for a variety of reasons. In only 10 of the states were the laws state-wide in operation. The decision to grant or refuse pensions lay generally in the hands of the counties. Even before the depression only about one-half of the counties had made use of their power to grant pensions. The increasing financial pressure of the depression has caused a steady decline in the number of counties paying them.

No state can obtain any help from the federal government unless it undertakes to make its mothers' pension plan state-wide, and to make it mandatory upon all the political subdivisions of the state. Only if they regard the financial help offered by the federal government as adequate will the states increase their budgets by extending pensions in this way, especially where the counties not now accepting the pensions law are poor counties, unable to put up much of the money. If the states anticipate that sooner or later the cost of maintaining the dependent children previously cared for under the Federal Emergency Relief Administration will be thrust back on the state budgets, they will probably find it worth while to set up a pensions plan meeting the federal government's requirements. At least a portion of the cost of keeping their dependent children can then be charged to the federal Treasury. But a larger subsidy would have been more effective in stimulating them to take this action.

Pensions are likely to be limited to children below the age of sixteen, for the federal government will pay no part of the cost of assistance to children above this age. The residence requirement is not so exacting as that in the old-age pension laws. The states may, to protect themselves from an influx of people seeking pensions, limit the right to a pension to those who have lived there for a certain period of time. Under the Social Security Act they may not, however, demand that any child shall have lived in the state for more than one year preceding the application for aid. If the child was born in the state within one year of application, its mother need not have resided in the state for more than one year immediately preceding the birth.

The money for pensions will be provided to the extent of one-third from federal and two-thirds from state funds, unless the states pay monthly pensions amounting to more than $18 for the first dependent child, and $12 for each succeeding child. In such a case more than two-thirds of the total expenditure must be raised by the states and their local authorities.

The final sharing of the burden of the cost of these pensions depends upon considerations similar to those discussed in connection with the old-age pensions. It depends, in other words, upon the taxes levied by federal and state governments to raise the necessary money. Little can be said about the ultimate source of the money provided by the federal government, although for reasons given in Chapter Nine, it is probable that at least part of it will be provided by the new taxes on payrolls and wages.

Each state has hitherto raised the money for mothers' pensions in its own way. We have seen that five-sixths of the funds raised by states in 1934 for these pensions were collected by the cities and counties. The county tax boards have, as a rule, been free to decide how to raise the money.

Security for Homeless and Neglected Children

The pensions for dependent children will help only those fortunate enough to have relatives who offer them a home. The 300,000 dependent homeless children in institutions and foster homes and those as yet uncared for, as well as those in danger of becoming delinquent, will be assisted by another part of the Security Act. Federal grants will be paid to states prepared to establish special child welfare services for these children. Each year a total sum of $1,500,000 will be available for this purpose.

A number of states have already attempted to protect abused and neglected children by setting up probation services in connection with juvenile courts, investigating foster homes and institutions claiming to care for abandoned children, and developing similar services. But this work has been crippled by lack of funds especially in the rural and depressed areas.

Each state can obtain under the Social Security Act a grant of $10,000 a year if its plans for spending the grant are approved by the United States Children's Bureau. The remainder of the money appropriated in the Act will be distributed among the states in proportion to their rural populations provided the states submit satisfactory programs.

Security for Widows

The widows of the country receive little additional security from the Social Security Act. They may benefit under at least four parts of the Act, but not very much from any of them. Widows who have been employed at any time in their lives in industries covered by the contributory old-age annuities plan will be entitled (in common with all the other contributors) to annuities in their own right when they reach the age of sixty-five. As the amount of these annuities is determined by the wages received and the number of years of employment, most married women will be entitled to very small benefits, for the wage earner's wife usually works for a relatively short time before marriage and scarcely at all afterwards. Her chances of being insured, even while at work, are, as we saw on page 27, much smaller than a man's because the employments most favored by women are largely excluded from the old-age annuities plan.

Widows may, however, benefit under the annuities plan if they share in their husband's estates. The estate of a man covered by old-age annuities may be increased under the Act in three ways: If a contributor dies before the age of sixty-five, 3½ per cent of the total wages paid to him after December 31, 1936, will be paid to his estate. If he dies after the age of sixty-five but before the total sum paid to him in annuities amounts to 3½ per cent of the total wages on which he has paid contributions, the difference is paid to his estate. Finally, if by some mistake he received during his life less than the correct annuity to which he was entitled, and the correct annuity was more than 3½ per cent of his total wages, the difference between what he received and what he should have obtained is paid to his estate.

The additional security a widow can hope for on account of these payments under the annuity plan will, therefore, depend upon the previous earnings of her husband, how long he works after he is sixty-five, the age at which he dies and whether or not he decides to cut her out of his will. It would be to her advantage to have married a man who had earned high wages or who had been paying contributions for a long period. Both these factors increase the total amount of wages, and, therefore, the 3½ per cent of that total. It will pay her to encourage her husband to continue to work as long as possible after the age of sixty-five. As he is not entitled to draw old-age annuities for any month in which he works beyond that age, she will have some present security from his earnings plus the knowledge that when he dies the maximum possible sum will be paid to his estate because he has drawn no annuity.

If her husband refuses or is unable to work after the age of sixty-five, but if he lives long enough to draw annuities equal to $3\frac{1}{2}$ per cent of the sum on which he paid the wage tax, she obtains nothing from the fund if she survives him. In any case, the prospective widow is never very secure, for her chance of obtaining the funds that may be due to her husband's estate depends upon the relations between her and her husband. If she quarrels with him or he is eccentric, he may leave the whole of the money to a home for lost cats.

Widows may, however, hope for increased security under the Act in a third way. They may obtain payments under the plans for aiding dependent children. Some part of these payments may be intended for the support of the person caring for the child. If so, the $18 and $12 benefits visualized by the Act are miserably inadequate. Unless the states will provide more than two-thirds of the cost of these pensions, a needy widow with two children must live upon $30 a month, a sum which the federal government evidently regards as an appropriate pension for elderly people whose needs are few. Moreover, when her children reach the age of sixteen the pension ceases and the widow is again penniless.

Finally, needy widows may hope, if they survive to the age of sixty-five, to obtain old-age pensions in at least a majority of the states. But here too the security falls short of what is required and it carries much of the stigma of the poor law. In any case, it is not available to widows under sixty-five years of age.

In other countries widows and orphans have been provided for through the social insurance system. Workers under such a survivors' insurance plan pay contributions during their working lives, and when they die their widows are entitled to a regular cash income, payable as a right and irrespective of need. Such plans usually pay pensions also to orphans until they reach a certain age. Sometimes widows obtain these annuities only if they are over sixty-five or if they are caring for young children. In other schemes the widow of a qualified contributor obtains an annuity regardless of age, until she remarries.

Summary

The needs of those whose customary bread-winner has died or deserted them are recognized in the Security Act. Federal grants will be made to the states to enable them to give more security to needy dependent children under sixteen years of age. Relatives who are willing to care for such children will receive monthly pensions up to $18 for the first and $12 for each additional child. These pensions will be paid on proof of need, but there is no obligation on the recipients to repay the pensions. No children will benefit unless the states pass laws approved by the Social Security Board. Many states may hesitate to meet the standards required by the Act because it will cost them money to do so and the financial inducement offered by the federal government is not very large.

Neglected children will benefit from the expenditure of $1,500,000 made available by the Act for assistance to homeless children and those in danger of becoming delinquent. But here too there will be no additional security unless the states are willing to develop programs that meet with the approval of the United States Children's Bureau.

Widows are poorly provided for, although they may benefit from four parts of the Act. The two kinds of security they may hope for under the annuities plan are very precarious, while they can obtain old-age pensions only if they are over sixty-five. Their share in the pensions paid for the care of dependent children will cease when the youngest child becomes sixteen. Many of them will by that time be too old to seek wage-earning employment (probably for the first time) with any prospects of success.

Chapter Seven

INDIVIDUAL SECURITY AND THE SOCIAL SECURITY ACT

T HOSE who have read the preceding chapters in the hope of discovering how far the Act increases the security of the average individual must have been impressed by two features: the strange unevenness of the achievement and the great variety in the methods of providing security.

Inequalities in the Security Provided

The money income which insecure people can expect varies in the different parts of the program. Aged people drawing annuities will receive incomes varying from $10 to $85 a month. Those granted old-age or blind pensions are likely to obtain $30 a month at most. Relatives caring for dependent children may receive monthly pensions up to $18 for the first, and $12 for each additional child. Unemployed workers are not guaranteed any minimum sum although in some states they may receive weekly benefits as high as 50 or even 65 per cent of their previous wages.

The relatively low level of the benefits provided will cause disappointment in many quarters. The $40 to $50 a month likely to be received by the average retired worker under the federal annuities plan, or the monthly pension of $30 under the state old-age pension laws, will seem to many to be very poor substitutes for the $200 a month which the Townsend plan promises to all aged people. Unemployment benefits amounting at best to 50 or 65 per cent of wages for 12 to 16 weeks cannot compare with benefits equal to total average past wages for the whole period of unemployment promised by the Lundeen or Workers' Bill, which was introduced into Congress in 1935.

It is evident that the scope of the security provided varies greatly from one field of insecurity to another. It most nearly approaches completeness in regard to old-age insecurity. The federal annuities and the federal-state old-age pensions together go far to remove from aging people the specter of dependency. But the annuities system, the more attractive of the two, will cover only about one-third of the adult population, and many of the annuities will be small. Those who obtain small annuities, or none at all, must rely upon old-age pensions which they will obtain only in the states that pass pension laws. Although in theory these pensions are superior to public welfare relief, they retain a number of relief features which will discourage the more sensitive of the aged poor from applying for them. A considerable part of the cost of maintaining the dependent aged will continue to fall upon the shoulders of their children.

In the remaining fields of insecurity there are great gaps due to the fact that many people are given no protection at all, or that protection when given is inadequate. Unemployment compensation is available only to workers in the small number of states setting up unemployment compensation plans. Only some of the workers in these states will be covered, and it is almost impossible to say how much benefit the unemployed will receive, and for how many weeks of unemployment they can count upon it. The Act is a very unpromising first step in the provision of security against unemployment.

The Social Security Act hardly touches insecurity due to ill health. The total of sickness will probably be diminished by increased expenditure by the federal and the state governments on public health services. But the resulting benefits will be diffused throughout the whole population. The expanded special health services authorized by the Act will greatly benefit mothers and children. Those blind persons who are in need will draw pensions in states passing the necessary laws. Disabled people may hope for advice and training. But in the future, as in the past, the ordinary person who falls sick must bear the full cost of his doctor's bills, his medicines and his hospital treatment. More important still, he will obtain no income at all for the days when sickness prevents him from working.

While the Security Act somewhat increases the security of those who depend upon the earnings of others for income, it still leaves them exposed to many risks. Dependent children, fortunate enough to live in states passing the necessary laws, will undoubtedly be better off in the future. More of them will obtain assistance and they will probably receive larger sums than in the past. But widows who cannot work because of age, or who should not work because they have to care for young children, receive little additional security. The former may receive death benefits under the old-age annuities plan, but these will never be very large. If their husbands live long after the age of sixty-five they will receive nothing. If their husbands worked in the occupations not covered by the annuity plan, they will have no rights at all. Young widows with children can hope only for the death benefit, which is likely to be small if their husbands die young, or for some share in the small pensions paid for dependent children by the states.

The dependents of unemployed workers in the lower wage brackets may even be worse off as a result of the Security Act. If the head of the family was employed in a trade covered by a state unemployment compensation system, unemployment benefits will, as a rule, not exceed 50 per cent of his earnings. Since only the District of Columbia plan provides for dependents' benefits, dependents will often receive less than under home relief, which usually takes account of the size of the family and its needs.

The benefits of the Act do not affect equally all groups in the population. Persons in agriculture, domestic service, state, and federal service, and those working for non-profit-making organizations, or on their own account, will get relatively little additional security. They are excluded from the important old-age annuity plan and from the unemployment compensation scheme. They will benefit somewhat from the remaining sections of the Act. Workers in small concerns will be at a disadvantage for they will receive no unemployment compensation. Men will benefit more than women, and white persons more than colored. Children will benefit more than other age groups from the health program.

Differences in the Methods of Providing Security

From whatever angle we regard the Security Act, it offers variety and diversity. The kinds of security provided differ widely. Sometimes security takes the form of free services, sometimes of the offer of cash. Sometimes the amount of the cash is determined by a man's previous earnings; sometimes it is dependent upon his needs. Security is also provided under different conditions. In the unemployment and old-age annuities plans the benefits will be given in the form of a right, and no questions will be asked about an individual's private means. In the various pension plans, benefits are limited to people who can prove that they are in need.

Two quite different methods of financing economic security are to be found in different parts of the Act. The pensions for the needy aged, for the blind, and for dependent children, and the cost of the health services are met out of general taxation. The contributory old-age annuities and the unemployment compensation plans will be financed out of special taxes. In the former case these taxes will be paid by employers and workers, in the latter by employers alone.

The responsibility accepted by the federal government also varies very greatly from one part of the program to another. The old-age annuities plan is exclusively federal. Unemployment compensation, mothers' pensions, pensions to the needy aged and to the blind, and the health services are administered partly by the federal but mainly by the state governments. Division of responsibility varies from one scheme to another. When the federal government places the major responsibility for action upon the states it uses two different methods to encourage them to act. In the unemployment compensation plan it adopts the device of taxing all employers and then permitting them to escape most of the federal tax if their states set up compensation plans of which the federal government approves. On the other hand, states are stimulated to assist dependent children, the aged, and the blind, and to embark on public health programs by a federal offer to share the cost under certain conditions.

Economic Security and the Existing Social Order

Why such diversity? Is there any justification for such differences in the coverage, kinds of benefits, and methods of financing in the various fields of economic insecurity? Is no simpler solution possible? Is the Social Security Act so varied and complex merely because politicians are perverse compromisers and bureaucrats live on and in red tape? These questions can be answered only if we are aware of the difficulties of setting up a security program. Legislators and administrators work, even when their will is good, within limitations. They must fit the program into a running economic society with all its established institutions, its prejudices, and traditions. Many of the complexities of the law arise out of these institutions and attitudes.

In the first place we are trying to give economic security to people living in a society organized on the assumption that there is no security. Our society relies upon the desire to obtain income as a means of compelling or persuading individuals to take part in production by selling their labor or renting their property. If we give them security without requiring in return active participation in production, we may take the mainspring out of the social machine. The conditions and restrictions which are attached to the benefits given in the various parts of the Act are intended to avoid this danger.

In the second place, we are trying to give security that inevitably costs money without having decided who should foot the bill. We rather loosely accept the belief that each person should pay for what he gets, and some of the most questionable parts of the Act are the result of attempts to raise the necessary money by this principle. But we have at least dimly realized that the most insecure people are too poor to pay for complete security. Hence in some parts of the Act we provide only such security as individuals can afford to pay for, and in others we reluctantly introduce a contribution from general taxation.

In the third place, we are attempting to provide security through governmental action and we have not one but 49 governments, to say nothing of the two territories. So at some points we must choose between the rights of the states to freedom of action and the rights of insecure individuals living in states which are unwilling or unable to provide a minimum of security. The Act is full of compromises between these conflicting interests.

Finally the American Constitution limits the use of federal governmental authority to provide economic security. Some of the devices adopted in the Security Act are due to the necessity of keeping within these limits.

Summary

The Social Security Act achieves a very uneven measure of success in protecting the individual against the major hazards to his economic security. The money incomes provided for different groups of insecure people vary considerably and are very modest in amount. The scope of the protection afforded varies from one field of insecurity to another. Different groups in the population receive a differing measure of protection. The aged are most completely provided for. The sick have gained least from the Act. Women and colored persons are to a large extent denied the opportunity to obtain some of the more desirable kinds of security.

There is an equally remarkable diversity in the methods of providing security. Both the form and the conditions of payment of benefits vary in the different plans. Two methods of providing the necessary money are adopted. The part played by the federal government varies from plan to plan. Where the federal government cooperates with the states two quite different devices are utilized to encourage the states to act.

The necessity for this variety in achievement and methods cannot be determined without some understanding of the fundamental difficulties facing those who attempt to provide economic security through governmental action. The attempt to develop an adequate and simple economic security program must be made in a world that relies upon economic insecurity to stimulate individuals to take part in production. It involves raising money in a society that has not yet squarely faced the issue as to who should pay for security. It must take account of the existence of 48 states, jealous of their right to experiment and to control their own domestic affairs. Finally the Constitution sets limits to the action which the federal government may take to bring about greater economic security.

Before we criticize the Social Security Act as inadequate and clumsy, we must discover how far its limitations and complications are the result of these very real difficulties and how far they are due to causes less deeply embodied in the very nature of our social order.

Chapter Eight

ECONOMIC SECURITY VERSUS RUGGED INDIVIDUALISM

THE economic world is governed by prices. Movements of prices regulate production. When there is less of a commodity than people want to buy at the current price, that price rises, and producers are encouraged to increase their output. When there is more of it than consumers will buy, the price falls. When prices fall, sellers must either accept this lower price if they wish to sell as much as before, or sell less if they insist on the old price.

This fundamental principle applies also to those who are seeking to obtain income by selling their labor for wages or lending their property for interest or rent. In times of prosperity, businessmen who believe they can make profits if they have commodities to sell bid against one another to secure the services of workers and the capital and land of property-owners without which they cannot produce. Wages and interest rates accordingly rise. But

132

when, as happens in a depression, businessmen can no longer sell at the same price as before, their demand for labor, land, and capital is less. Workers and property owners too must offer what they have to sell at a lower price if they wish to dispose of as much as before.

This pressure on would-be sellers to accept the market price on pain of not selling at all takes place at all times. If consumers decide they prefer rayon clothing to cotton, the price of cotton goods falls. Workers and businessmen engaged in the production of cotton goods must either accept lower wages and profits or move to trades making the products for which people are willing to pay a higher price.

Our economic order rests upon private property. It is of the essence of private property that what a man owns cannot be taken away from him by force. Those who desire to consume goods and services owned by other people must, instead of seizing them, offer something in exchange. If they own property they can sell or lend it to others in exchange for the goods and services they require to meet their daily needs. If they have no property, they can sell only their labor. If they cannot sell their labor, they cannot consume because they have nothing to offer in return for the goods and services they require.

133

Between 85 and 90 per cent of the population do not possess enough property to live upon without working. Workers are thus especially sensitive to this pressure to change employments or accept lower wages when the demand for their services falls off. Failure to sell their labor, which means failure to obtain a job, spells quick starvation. Workers cannot afford to hold out indefinitely in the hope that wages will rise to the old level or that the demand for their services will revive.

This pressure on workers quickly to change their wage demands or their occupations when unemployment begins is a very important factor in our economic life. It helps to give our economic system that quality which economists call *flexibility*. In other words, when production ceases because people find they have been producing the wrong things or because of a disagreement between the people taking part in production as to the price each should get for his services, the pressure of fear of loss of income compels them to reach a speedy agreement in order once more to take part in production. Anything which makes it possible for workers or property owners to hold out against a reduction of the price of what they have to sell postpones this adjustment. If no production takes place everyone suffers.

Rugged individualism pushed to its logical extreme thus means that only those who contribute to production obtain any share in what is produced. No share in production means no income, and no income means starvation. Economic insecurity is the mainspring of the system.

This method of persuading or coercing the majority of the population to produce is crude and unsatisfactory in many ways. But it cannot be abandoned without substituting some equally effective stimulus to work. Will people be willing to cooperate in production and do what may often be unpleasant jobs, under conditions which they may dislike, in return for anything other than the offer of a material reward? Both Russia and Germany have discovered at least a partial alternative in the form of love of one's fellow men or one's class, or the sense of duty to the state. But until American society is so changed that people will be willing to cooperate in production for such idealistic reasons, we must retain our present driving force for want of something better.

Every departure from rugged individualism involves some loss of the flexibility of our economic system. Economic security is such a departure, for it means giving people income regardless of their contribution to production. The nearer the guaranteed income approaches

135

that which could be obtained by working at prevailing wages, the less the inducement to work at what the individual considers an inadequate remuneration, or in employments different from those to which he has been accustomed. The more adequate the income he is assured in old age, the less may he strive to save up enough capital to support his declining years.

The failure to recognize the first of these dilemmas was one of the great weaknesses of the Lundeen or Workers' Unemployment Insurance Bill. This Bill, which was introduced into Congress in 1935 and received wide support, would have guaranteed to all would-be wage earners a money income equal to the average wages in their district so long as they were willing to work but unable to do so through no fault of their own. Such a guarantee is incompatible with the present economic order. It removes the means of persuading or coercing workers into accepting lower wages, if this should be necessary. Workers in private industry who were paid at less than the local average wage would be better off if they left their jobs. By doing so they would raise the local average still higher and induce more to leave their jobs. This difficulty was undoubtedly seen by some of the supporters of the Lundeen Bill. Many of them would even claim that its tendency to disrupt the existing individualistic profit-making order was one of its most appealing qualities.

Departures from Rugged Individualism

Rugged individualism is, however, nowhere pushed to its logical limits. Individuals who neither toil nor spin do obtain incomes. People physically unable to work and without enough property to yield an adequate income are supported by charitable societies, public pensions, or relief. We explain these exceptions to the general rule by reflecting that we are not seriously interfering with the productive system because these individuals could not cooperate in production under any circumstances.

We do not allow the families of unemployed workers to remain without income until their breadwinner is compelled by the whip of starvation to accept any kind of job, at any kind of wage. More of the ruggedness of individualism is thus sacrificed. This exception is defended on the ground that it is not fair to punish young children and their mothers because of the unwillingness or inability of their breadwinners to support them.

Even in dealing with able-bodied breadwinners who might be expected to work for their income, we hesitate to apply the pressure of loss of income to the bitter limit. We are too squeamish to allow people to die of starvation even though we may believe they are asking an unreasonable wage as the price of their cooperation in production. We contribute to community chests and develop city and state and federal relief organizations to prevent potential workers and their families from starving while the pressure is making itself felt. Again we find good arguments for thus breaking the basic rule of our economic order. In a severe depression many workers can find no jobs even though they tramp unceasingly and are willing to accept any offer. The humanitarian argues that such suffering is too great a price to pay for a flexible economic order resulting in high efficiency of production. To give food without work may reduce flexibility but the reduction must be cheerfully borne in order to set bounds to human misery. Those callous enough to be unmoved by the degradation and suffering of poverty are still not insensitive to the danger of political explosion where there are numbers of desperate people. The destitute and hopeless may prefer death at the barricades to death in the gutter. A minimum of security may thus be the price that our capitalist society has to pay to ensure its own survival.

Individual Guarantees and Social Safeguards

But so long as we retain the individualistic system of production for profit any social security program must be designed so as not to interfere *unduly* with that system. The economic order can be protected in at least four ways even though individuals are assured a minimum of security. Firstly, security may be given under conditions so unpleasant that it will be accepted only in emergency. Secondly, the standard of living assured may be so much lower than that obtainable by taking an active part in production that individuals will still find it worth while to try to obtain more money. Thirdly, more adequate security may be granted under more pleasant conditions only to carefully selected groups who prove that they have cooperated in production in the past. Finally, the period for which security is granted may be limited so that the threat of loss of income operates as soon as the period is over. The Social Security Act utilizes all these safeguards.

The principle that publicly provided security should be unpleasant is the most venerable of these devices. The public welfare systems which stand between the incomeless individual and starvation have always given assistance as grudgingly and unpleasantly as possible. They

139

usually assure only the bare necessities of life. The price of this meager security in several states is the loss of the right to vote. Public assistance is everywhere given only to those who can prove that they have no other resources and no relatives who might support them. It is given only to paupers. Often it is provided only if the needy person will perform certain test work to prove that he is genuinely willing to work if given the opportunity.

The last few years have revealed the unsatisfactoriness of this safeguard, especially as a way of providing for the millions who are unemployed through no fault of their own. The self-respecting worker who has accumulated savings can obtain no help until he has exhausted his resources and become a pauper, while his shiftless neighbor who never saved at all obtains assistance as soon as he is unemployed. Yet no more satisfactory substitute has been adopted. Indeed, the Social Security Act retains the device. Old-age assistance is given only to persons over sixty-five who are in need. Need is still interpreted to mean lack of relatives able to provide support. The aged who have frugally saved up a small property are denied pensions if their savings are more than a certain small sum. In many states the pensions are still given grudgingly. The grants to the blind and to those caring for dependent children will be restricted to applicants who can prove that they "need" assistance. The needy aged, the blind, or guardians of dependent children who are unwilling to face the task of displaying their poverty sufficiently to convince the public investigating officer will obtain no benefits under the Social Security Act. This condition may be reasonable but it will undoubtedly deter many sensitive but deserving people from seeking public aid. These sections of the Act have been, with some justification, described as nothing more than a somewhat generous and glorified poor relief.

The second device for protecting our productive organization against the dangers of guaranteeing security is to fix benefits much below what people could earn in employment. The benefits provided by state unemployment schemes seldom exceed 50 per cent of wages, and may, indeed, fall much below this level. But although the spur to work is thus retained, the use of this safeguard raises new difficulties. Most wage earners in the lower ranks can scarcely live upon their full-time earnings. How then will they manage on 50 per cent or less of this sum? Obviously, even under these new schemes, they will fail to obtain adequate security.

Undoubtedly the most novel parts of the Social Security Act are those which make use of

141

the third protective device. The social insurance principle used in the contributory old-age annuities and the unemployment compensation systems provides economic security, under relatively pleasant conditions, to limited groups of carefully selected people. Under the social insurance principle benefits are given as a right (and not as a grudging concession) to workers who have paid contributions (or for whom contributions have been paid by their employers) for not less than a certain number of weeks.

This restriction of the more pleasant kinds of security to people selected in this way has undeniable advantages. The fact of having worked for the prescribed number of weeks in the past suggests that the individual is one who normally intends to make his living by cooperating in production. The perpetually tired and those who work only in spurts cannot claim this kind of security because they will be unable to satisfy the so-called "contributory" condition.

This limitation of security to people who have been wage earners for a considerable period has, however, the disadvantage that it limits the *scope* of security. Those who have not been wage earners, for example, housewives, and all those who (like many professional people) work independently, get no protection. Our discussion of the unemployment and the contributory old-age

142

annuities system showed, however, that the classes of people excluded from benefit was wider even than this. Many of these additional exclusions are due to the difficulties of administering a plan based on the social insurance principle. Records must be kept of the contributors and machinery devised to ensure that contributions are paid by all those liable to do so. Otherwise it will be impossible to decide who is entitled to benefits. Since workers change their employers and move about from place to place, these payments must be checked week by week. The more we try to preserve the spirit of individualism by relating the amount of security given under the social insurance plan to the earnings a man has received in the past, the more difficult becomes the task of administration. The old-age annuities plan will necessitate keeping records of each worker's earnings for every year of his working life. If we followed the example of other countries and gave a uniform annuity to all workers paying a uniform annuities tax, no such detailed and lengthy records would be necessary.

Since our method calls for a complicated administrative machine, the more inclusive the coverage of the plan to begin with, the more overwhelming the job of setting up this system. It has, therefore, been thought wise to limit, at least to begin with, the groups of people who receive this kind of security. Workers in agriculture and in domestic service in a private home have been excluded from both unemployment compensation and contributory old-age annuities largely for this reason. Both these classes of workers are widely scattered and the number of employers in relation to workers is very much greater than in most other occupations. Thus the collection of taxes would be more troublesome.

These differences may be overcome in the future and some of them are probably exaggerated. Many other countries have found it possible to include both agriculture and domestic service in contributory old-age annuities systems. Nor does there seem any reason why at least agriculture and perhaps also domestic service might not in time be included under the unemployment compensation plan. If we do not do so there is a danger that workers may shun those employments which disqualify them for security benefits. It has been found in Great Britain, where these same employments have been excluded from the unemployment compensation system, that workers are unwilling to enter them because they lose their rights to security.

The social insurance method of protecting society against malingerers thus involves many exclusions from security. But it is not responsible for all the exclusions found in the Social Security Act. There is no reason, apart from political pressure exercised by representatives of the employers concerned, why workers in the employment of religious, charitable, scientific, literary, and educational organizations should be denied unemployment compensation or old-age annuities.

The exclusion from unemployment compensation plans of workers whose employers employ less than eight workers is even more difficult to justify. The argument that administration will be especially difficult is not very convincing, especially when we remember that they are included in the contributory old-age annuities scheme where the same problems arise. The disadvantages of this distinction between large and small employers are obvious. It will greatly complicate the administration of the unemployment compensation plan. There will be endless possibilities for dispute as to whether an employer is or is not liable to pay the tax. Employers who employ eight or nine workers will be tempted to discharge workers to bring their staff below the limit set in the law. They will attempt to meet extra orders by working overtime and overburdening their existing employees instead of taking on additional workers who would render them liable to the tax.

The exclusion of the small concerns will also be unfair to workers, who will be compelled to shun employment with such firms if they wish to retain their right to unemployment compensation benefits in the future. It will be difficult to explain to them why they will be covered if their employer has eight workers but not if he has seven. Are they to be denied benefits for refusing to accept a job with a small employer when they know that by doing so they cut themselves off from the chance of unemployment benefits in the future?

The last of the devices by which we attempt to give security without endangering the running of our economic machine is to put a limit to the time for which security is given. We might give people unemployment compensation benefits for only a limited number of weeks. During this period they could not be pressed to take jobs other than those to which they were accustomed, or at wages less than going wages.

Such a relaxation of the pressure to accept employment at lower wages for the first few weeks of unemployment may even be of advantage to society as a whole. If the falling off in demand in a worker's own trade is only temporary, it is obviously wasteful to compel him to learn other work if he will soon be needed again in his old job. It is not always possible to know

146

whether an increase in unemployment is the sign of a depression for which the only remedy is a reduction in the general level of wages. If the depression is short-lived and due to causes unconnected with the level of wages, it may not pay to bring pressure on workers to accept lower wages when the old wage level will prevail as soon as business revives. After several weeks it may be easier to tell whether or not it is necessary to press workers to take jobs at lower wages.

The laws of the various states which have set up unemployment compensation programs usually give benefits for a maximum of 15 or 16 weeks. But here too society is protected at the expense of limiting the security given. The proportion of the unemployed who have been out of work more than 15 weeks is by no means negligible. In periods of depression many workers are out of work for two, three, or even four years. The problem of providing economic security for those unemployed for more than 15 or 16 weeks remains untouched. In spite of the tremendous progress made in building up the Federal Emergency Relief Administration and developing the public works and the work relief programs, this problem still awaits a satisfactory solution. If the contributory unemployment compensation program is a satisfactory way of

147

dealing with the unemployed, it seems reasonable to ask whether it is economical to build up such expensive machinery for restricting benefits to the right people if the machinery is to be used only for 15 weeks. On the other hand if we believe that America cannot run the risk of workers refusing jobs at less than going wages for longer than 15 weeks, the limit must stay where it is.

The Legitimate Sphere of Private Enterprise

The desire to preserve the individualistic system of production complicates the provision of economic security in yet another way. If security is given in the form of money payments, our main concern, as we have seen, is with the effects of this guarantee of income on the willingness of the recipient to participate in production. But if the government gives security in the form of jobs or by providing services, there are new difficulties—the dangers of encroaching upon the opportunity of private producers to make profits.

The omission of any provision for work relief in the Security Act is in part due to the many difficulties inherent in this way of dealing with unemployment. These concern both the wages paid for such work and the kinds of work to be done. The government cannot pay wages equal only to ordinary relief. Work relief employees would be penalized by the additional wear and

148

tear on clothes and the cost of the extra food they would need. If the government pays wages equal to those paid by private enterprise it is criticized for keeping up wages in a depression and thus making it difficult for private concerns to sell cheaply and so bring about revival. If it pays wages less than prevailing rates it is criticized by organized labor for sweating workers and setting a bad example to private employers. Work at wages only slightly above relief payments is not meeting unemployment by providing jobs as workers understand the word.

The choice of appropriate work projects is equally difficult. If the relief workers produce useful goods consumed by the ordinary man the government is charged with taking business away from private employers. If it uses the workers to carry out the normal functions of government it is accused of trying to get its work done cheaply and at the expense of ordinary full-time workers. If, in avoiding the toes of private profit-makers it produces things that the ordinary man would not be willing to pay for it is charged with "boondoggling."

Work relief has undoubtedly a part to play in a complete security program. But it must probably be limited to those cases where the unemployed need it most, and where its economic advantages to the rest of the community are greatest. It is doubtful whether at the present time we have adequately explored all its implications or are in a position to decide its place in a permanent program. In the face of these difficulties Congress was wise in not writing into the Social Security Act any provision for work relief.

The attempt to protect the individual from the hazards of ill health through some form of social insurance has been opposed by two groups, insurance companies and medical men, both speaking in the spirit of individualism. It is easier to understand than to sympathize with the point of view of the first group. Government provision of insurance against sickness costs is opposed on the grounds that it dangerously limits the sphere of activity of the private insurance companies. It is the thin end of a dangerous wedge. Yet private companies have never seriously attempted to provide health insurance on a large scale and would probably find it a difficult and unprofitable enterprise.

The opposition of the medical profession has a more solid and respectable basis. The relationship between doctor and patient is an intensely personal one and perhaps for this reason doctors tend to be strong individualists. They cannot see how such a personal service could be provided on a large scale by governmental action. It is, of course, more difficult to ensure that a sick man receives proper care and treatment and is not dealt with in a perfunctory manner than it is to see that he obtains an old-age annuity of the right amount. But the experience of other countries has shown that it is possible, by the use of insurance, to provide for individual treatment without making a medical practitioner a state employee. The problem of ensuring that the doctor provides as good service when he is paid a uniform sum per patient as he does when he is paid roughly in proportion to the income of his patients and the time spent on each should not be beyond the capacity of the medical profession to solve. No profession gives more unstintingly of its time to those who are sick but impoverished, or has a finer tradition of public service.

Summary

Many of the shortcomings of the Social Security Act which were noted in previous chapters are due to the necessity of preventing the guarantee of security from undermining an individualistic society. To avoid a dangerous weakening of the stimulus to cooperate in production we give security under rather unpleasant conditions. We provide benefits well below what a man could obtain by working. We use the social insurance principle to limit the more pleasant forms of security to those who can prove they are workers. Finally we give security only for a limited time. If we are fearful of weakening the mainspring of our economic order we must not grumble because the security afforded by the Act is limited to people who are needy, is meager in amount, confined to those who have been wage earners in the past, or provided only for a limited period. The exclusion of employees of non-profit-making concerns and of those whose employers have seven or fewer workers, cannot, however, be explained in these terms, while the exclusion of such employments as agriculture and domestic service from the old-age and unemployment compensation programs should be only temporary. But with these exceptions we can widen the scope of the security we offer or make it more generous only if we are prepared to pay the price in terms of a slightly less elastic and flexible economic order.

In the same way if we cling to the belief that there are some fields of activity which the government should never enter, we must not complain because the security we provide takes the form of the payment of cash rather than the offer of work or the provision of services.

Chapter Nine

FINANCING ECONOMIC SECURITY

ECONOMIC security costs money. If people
live without income or savings it must
be at the expense of others. This expense may
be met by relatives or friends who give money
or supply food and shelter. It may be borne by
shopkeepers and others who extend credit that
is never repaid. The burden may be carried by
landlords who cannot collect rent from tenants
without income and yet hesitate to evict them
immediately they fall into arrears. It may be
carried by consumers who pay sales taxes to
provide funds for keeping the unemployed.
Finally, the cost may be shared by all the taxpayers of the country if Congress votes funds
for relief. The cost of providing security does
not disappear because we cannot say at any
moment who pays it.

In contrast to the haphazard methods of
distributing the costs of such security as is now
provided, the Social Security Act attempts to
distribute the cost in a more orderly manner.

153

The future cost of old-age security has been estimated within rough limits and definite plans made for sharing that cost among workers, employers, and the general public. The same kind of decision has been made about the cost of the first few weeks of unemployment compensation benefits. In future certain sums will be spent on pensions for the blind and for dependent children and for the promotion of public health. Under the Social Security Act the federal and state governments will share the cost of this kind of security in specified proportions.

The decision as to who should pay for economic security is perhaps the most difficult of all those to be made when security is provided. We can appear to avoid this decision by distributing the costs in such a disorderly manner that no one knows who really bears the burden. But as soon as we seek more orderly methods this unpleasant question can no longer be evaded. We must decide whether the cost should be borne by workers and those who are insecure or whether some share should be paid by people who have higher incomes and greater security. The desire to avoid the question is understandable. It is comforting to believe that there is a painless device for providing the money. In fact, however, there is no anaesthetic permitting the painless extraction of money from pockets.

The Social Security Act proposes to raise the money for economic security by two quite different methods. On the one hand, the money for old-age annuities and unemployment compensation is to be raised by a form of social insurance. Money will be collected from the employers of workers subject to the risks of old-age insecurity or unemployment. In the old-age annuities plan workers themselves will also contribute. On the other hand, the funds to finance the remaining parts of the security program are to be provided by the states and the federal government out of general taxation. What are the relative advantages of these two methods?

Self-sustaining Social Insurance

President Roosevelt, in making public the report of the Committee on Economic Security, said that social insurance was a sound and workable plan for providing economic security. He added that the system adopted, except for the money necessary to initiate it, should be "self-sustaining." By this he meant that funds for the payment of benefits should not come out of general taxation. In other words, the entire costs of the old-age annuities and unemployment compensation benefits must be provided by taxes on employers and workers.

155

There is, of course, a great deal to be said for providing economic security on the same basis as private insurance. If everyone contributes toward the cost, the burden on each individual can often be reduced. More protection can be given for the same amount of money. If all workers or their employers contribute to provide unemployment benefits the lucky help to pay for the unlucky.

It also seems reasonable (so long as we forget the low level of many incomes) that each person should save or insure for his own old age or unemployment, and that if he refuses, the state should compel him to do so. In this way it may prevent him from becoming a public charge in the future. We have already seen that by limiting security to people who have thus insured themselves, we can, to a large extent, protect society from people who have no intention of taking part in production if they can avoid it.

There is much to be said for collecting contributions from employers although this can hardly be called insurance, since the risk of loss of income falls not on them but on their workers. Employers, it is said, like to be able to hire and fire workers whenever they wish. Since the unemployed workers must exist during these periods in which there is no work, it seems fair that employers should pay at least a part of the

cost of keeping their workers alive during
slack periods. Many people believe that employers are largely responsible for unemployment, and hope that if they are saddled with
its costs they may try to organize their plants
so as to provide more regular work. It is also
argued that employers may fairly be asked to
contribute toward the cost of old-age annuities
because they obtain the benefits of a worker's
labor when he is young but have no use for him
as soon as he becomes old or sickly.

Who Pays for "Self-sustained" Security?

The most striking aspect of these arguments
in favor of financing social security by contributions from employers and workers is the
absence of any mention of the way in which this
method will distribute the costs of security
between the rich and the poor. Yet we can
hardly decide whether the self-sustaining social
insurance principle is a good one without con-
sidering the final distribution of the burden.

Unfortunately, however, it is by no means
easy to discover where these costs will ultimately
fall. Workers who must contribute 3 per cent
of their wages toward the cost of old-age annuities must bear their part of the burden. They
cannot pass it on to anyone else. But who finally

pays the 3 per cent contributed by the employer to the old-age annuities plan and the 3 per cent tax paid for the unemployment compensation scheme? No one knows.

Undoubtedly employers will do their best to pass this cost on to the consumer by charging higher prices. The larger the proportion of all employers paying this kind of tax, the easier will it be for them to add it to their selling prices. In the ordinary way it would be dangerous for any single employer to increase his prices because he would be afraid that his competitors would undersell him. But when the costs of all employers arc increased by this tax, the employer who adds the 6 per cent to his selling price is less likely to be undercut by his rivals. Since the costs of his rivals have been increased they could undercut only by paying at least part of the 6 per cent out of profits. They will not sacrifice profit in this way if they can help it. Hence the employers' share of the cost of the old-age annuities plan is likely sooner or later to be passed on to consumers. It will be more difficult, however, for employers to shift the burden of the unemployment compensation plan in the same way. The tax for old-age annuities applies to all manufacturing and commercial firms, but the tax for unemployment compensation is not payable by the small employers.

Those who are subject to the latter tax will therefore hesitate to raise their prices correspondingly for fear of the competition of the small employers who, not paying the tax, can sell at the same prices as before and still make profits.

The fact that the full 6 per cent tax for unemployment and old-age benefits will be paid only at the end of a number of years will make it easier to shift the burden to buyers. Consumers might protest against a sudden increase in prices but will probably scarcely notice a slow rise over 12 years. The increase in price will not be the same for all commodities. It will probably be greatest in those where little machinery and a great deal of labor is used in turning out the product. It will be easiest to squeeze the consumer in trades selling goods, such as necessities, that people cannot easily go without.

It is sometimes said that the payroll tax will be "pyramided," which means that the final consumer will pay it many times over if he buys goods that have passed through several firms in the process of production. In fact, the tax will no more be pyramided than the cost of labor. At each stage the tax is paid only on the payrolls at that stage. The total tax included in the final price of any article will thus not exceed 6 per cent on the sum total of all the wages paid for making it. In this respect a tax on payrolls differs from a sales or turnover tax which is levied on the *total value* of an article. This value, of course, includes the taxes paid on every previous occasion on which it or any of its constituents changed hands. Furthermore, the raw materials and labor used in making and distributing the article are taxed as many times as the product is sold.

Even if employers cannot pass the burden to consumers, they may shift it to the shoulders of workers. They may reduce wages or at least not increase them when trade revives as much as they would otherwise have done. This also will be more successful in some trades than in others. It will be most difficult in the industries where there are strong trade unions. It will be easiest in the lowest paid and least well-organized trades.

What kind of distribution of cost will then result from our efforts to finance security by the self-sustaining social insurance principle? It looks as if in the last resort workers will carry a great deal of the cost of their own security. If they are keen business men employers will certainly try to shift this cost either forward to purchasers or backward to workers. If the employer is able to shift the tax at all, the worker is bound to suffer. If it results in lower wages, his pay envelope will contain less. If the tax leads to higher prices, he will buy less with its contents.

If we agree with President Roosevelt that the self-sustaining social insurance method is the only sound way of financing annuities and unemployment compensation benefits, we are therefore saying that we believe that the poor should be compelled to pay most of the cost of helping the poor. The only escape from this result is to provide some of the money to finance security, even when given as a right, by general taxation which does not fall so heavily upon the poor.

Limited Scope of "Self-sustained" Security

Quite apart from the way in which it distributes the cost of security between the rich and the poor, the self-sustaining social insurance principle, which plays so large a part in the Security Act, has a number of other undesirable consequences. It enforces a limitation of the scope and the amount of the security given. Furthermore the very attempt to make sure that the money is provided solely by taxes on employers and workers raises difficult economic problems.

The difficulties of collecting contributions and of keeping records of the amount paid by each person leads (as we saw in the preceding chapter) to the exclusion of some groups of workers from the plan. If the amount of security given to workers is limited to what they or their employers have paid for, security is restricted still further. The worker who obtains only two or three days of casual work a week can hardly be expected to contribute to an old-age annuity out of his scanty earnings. The agricultural worker who earns $20 a month and his board can hardly contribute to such a plan without an unbearable reduction in his already low standard of living.

There are three ways of meeting the dilemma that those people who most need security are as a rule least able to pay for it. We may exclude such people entirely from the right to the more desirable forms of economic security; we may hold on to our principle and give them benefits, but only in proportion as they have contributed; or we may give everyone a certain minimum of security, and, where the money required to give this cannot be collected from the people themselves or their employers, make up the difference in some other way.

The Social Security Act adopts the first of these devices when it excludes agricultural and domestic workers from the old-age annuities and the unemployment compensation plans. But in order not to leave them entirely unprovided for when they are old it sets up the old-age assistance plan to give them poverty pensions if they are in need. If we insist that each person must pay for his own security when that security takes the form of a right to certain benefits, we shall always need some second method of dealing with those who cannot afford to pay for adequate security but who are not to be allowed to starve.

The second way out of the dilemma is adopted in the unemployment compensation plan. As the plans are to be self-supporting, the amount and the duration of unemployment benefits must be determined by the amount of money that can be raised by taxes on employers and workers. If, as seems likely, most states levy a tax on employers alone, they will be able to pay full benefits only for about 12 weeks. As a result the security they can give will be greatly restricted. Some other way of providing for those out of work for more than 12 weeks must be found.

Rigid adherence to the self-sustaining principle is also responsible for the fact that the old-age annuity to which the average worker can look forward will be about $45 although even the poverty pensions for a man and wife would by the standards of the Act itself amount to $60 a month.

The third way of meeting the dilemma is followed in another part of the old-age annuities plan. If people obtained annuities exactly in proportion to the sums paid by them or on their behalf, those who were already old when the Act came into effect would have contributed little by the time they were sixty-five. The annuities to which they would be entitled would amount to only a few cents a week. It would have been difficult to have offered such a plan to the millions of aging people and to have persuaded them that they were getting any real economic security. People who are already old and also those whose incomes are very low will therefore be given "unearned annuities," that is to say annuities considerably larger than they would be entitled to on the basis of their contributions.

Someone must pay for these unearned annuities. It was originally proposed that the federal government should pay for them out of general taxation. This is what has been done in other countries. But this plan did not commend itself to the Treasury, and ran counter to President Roosevelt's own wish for a self-sustaining insurance system. It was decided that the higher paid and the younger contributors should pay the cost.

While each person is assured of getting out of the old-age annuities fund at least what he has paid in wage taxes, those who pay for the longest time and earn the highest wages, will not (as we saw in Chapter Two) draw proportionately larger annuities. Part of the employers' contribution, which they might otherwise have shared, is used to pay for the unearned annuities of the older and lower paid workers. But we have also seen that a considerable part of the tax the employer has to pay will directly or indirectly be passed on to workers. Thus the cost of unearned annuities for the aged will ultimately be borne by people in the lower income groups, for the plan applies only to workers earning less than $3,000 a year, and to the first $3,000 of income of the relatively small number of people whose earnings are more than this amount. If it is a good plan to ask the young or higher paid wage earners to pay for the unearned annuities of their old or lower paid fellow workers, why not extend the principle further? Why draw the line at incomes of $3,000?

Economic Difficulties of a "Self-sustained" Security

The self-sustaining principle not only limits the scope and amount of protection given and concentrates the cost on the lower income groups. It also gives rise to a number of economic difficulties. There are, as we have seen, many arguments in favor of collecting at least part of the costs of social security from employers. But we must never forget that there are limits to the extent to which they can be saddled with the costs of security. The experience of other countries with various forms of social insurance, and of the states with workmen's compensation insurance, shows that it is possible to place some additional burden on employers without causing them to discharge workers. When they all have to pay the tax they can (as we saw above) shift it to someone else. Given time to adjust, they are able to pass the burden on to consumers and workers. Thus their own profits do not suffer. But the greater and more sudden the burden the more difficult is this shifting, and the greater the dislocation it involves. The Social Security Act recognizes this difficulty by providing that the full 3 per cent taxes for old-age pensions and for unemployment compensation shall be imposed only gradually.

But the present Act makes possible unemployment benefits for 12 to 15 weeks at most and gives no security at all to those who have no income because of sickness. Nor does it provide income as a right to widows or to the wives of aged workers. A more adequate job might require not a 6 per cent but a 12 per cent tax on payrolls. A considerable proportion of this tax would have to be imposed at once. If we spread out the 12 per cent taxes as the Act now spreads the 6 per cent taxes, it would be 24 years before the full tax was being paid. But people want security here and now. The economic disturbances due to the efforts of producers to increase prices or hold down wages might be so great that it would be simpler to provide some of the money out of general taxation. For while people grumble about paying income and sales taxes, their efforts to avoid them do not disturb the economic order as much as the efforts of employers to avoid payroll taxes. And we must not forget that one way in which employers can escape a tax on payrolls is to use more machinery and less labor.

The self-sustaining principle is clearly no final solution to the problem of distributing the cost of economic security. There is yet another reason why we should pause before accepting it. In the course of making it possible for people with low incomes to provide for their own security, the Act has been compelled to resort to financial devices that will involve us in grave economic and political difficulties. This danger faces us in the old-age annuities plan. The burden of providing adequate annuities for workers now young and for those already old will be heavy for both workers and employers. To make it more bearable the Social Security Act adopts a device familiar to those who save privately against old age. Individuals try to build up a sum of money which will yield interest that can be used as income when they are old. In the same way, to avoid collecting from employers and workers more than a total of 6 per cent at any time, the Security Act builds up a tremendous savings fund or reserve. It obtains the money by taxing more heavily in the first years than would be necessary if each worker had to pay only for his own security. This sum of money will be so great that by 1980 the interest will meet the cost of about 40 per cent of the annuities then falling due.

This use of private insurance methods will sidestep some of the unpleasant questions that would certainly arise if an attempt were made to collect more than 6 per cent from employers and workers. It saves the federal government from the anguish of making any contribution. But a reserve fund, which will grow to nearly twice the size of our present national debt, may be an embarrassing offspring of the Act. Future governments may find it difficult to keep this sum intact because most workers will fail to understand why, if the reserve is so tremendous, higher annuities cannot be paid. They will be pressed to hand out a little here and a little there, since a sum of nearly 50 billion dollars in federal hands will cause many palms to itch. It will also be difficult to find enough safe investments for so huge a sum. Changes in money market practices will be called for if all of the bonds issued by the federal government come to be held by the Old-age Reserve Account. The Treasury may find that the only way to invest so tremendous a sum with safety will be to lend it to the federal government in return for a promise to repay it later. The Act indeed gives power to invest in exactly this way.

Thus insistence on the self-sustaining principle in the Social Security Act may mean that all the people earning less than $3,000 a year will pay in the future a larger part than before of the current expenses of government. This state of affairs could be avoided by eliminating the large reserve. But the federal government would then have to supply now or in the future that part of the cost of the annuities to be provided under the present plan by the interest on the reserve. And this it cannot do without abandoning the rule that young people must pay for their own old-age security (and also that of the people already too old to provide for their own).

Financing Security out of General Taxation

Even if we abandon the idea of a self-sustaining insurance method of providing the money, we still face the problem of deciding who is to put up the money that will come out of general taxation. Under the Social Security Act the federal and state governments will provide funds for the non-contributory old-age pensions, for the pensions to dependent children and the blind, and for the various health services. Yet even here we cannot say who finally will bear the burden. Everything will depend on the kinds of taxes levied by the federal and the state governments.

It is only too probable that a considerable part of the money required by the federal government will come directly or indirectly out of the taxes paid by employers and workers under the Security Act. There are two ways in which the federal government will obtain additional income from the taxes paid by employers of eight or more workers which it can use to meet its obligations under other parts of the Act. In the first place, the taxes paid by such employers will be paid into the Federal Treasury as part of the ordinary internal revenue collections. They will flow into the special Unemployment Trust Fund only when the states set up plans and themselves collect taxes. By the end of 1935 only nine states and the District of Columbia had set up such plans. But since employers all over the country must pay the 3 per cent tax even if their states do not set up compensation funds, the federal government will for some time be receiving a tremendous additional income from employers in states that take no action, which it does not have to pay into the Unemployment Trust Fund.

In the second place the federal government will probably get some income over and above the minimum 0.3 per cent which all employers have to pay even if every state in the Union sets up an unemployment compensation fund. This will happen because the federal 3 per cent tax is levied on all wages and salaries regardless of their amount. But the state plans as a rule exclude workers with incomes over a certain sum (amounting usually to $2,500 or $3,000 a year). Since employers avoid paying 90 per cent of the federal tax only if they are paying an equivalent amount to their state fund, they will still have to pay the full 3 per cent federal tax on the salaries of their higher paid employees who are not covered in the state plans.

The federal government may decide to borrow the money required to finance security benefits. The large sums coming forward every year from the taxes on employers and workers to form the Old-age Reserve Account will, as we have seen, be very useful for this purpose. The federal government can spend the money and give in return a government bond promising to repay at a later date what it has borrowed. Since the tremendous size of the reserve will make it difficult to find suitable and safe investments, it is highly probable that the federal government will borrow the money in this way and use it, among other things, to meet its increased social security bill. No one can say what will happen after 1980 when the whole of the 3 per cent taxes on employers and workers will be needed to pay for the current annuities and the government must raise in some other way not merely the full cost of its own share of the security bill but also interest on its immense borrowings. Since this problem is so far off, it is probable that no one cares. The fact remains that for many years to come the money to pay for the federal government's share of the additional security given by the Act is likely to be provided out of the new taxes on employers and workers.

If the federal government obtains in the end no extra income as a result of the new taxes levied by the Act, and if it does not borrow from the Old-age Reserve Account, it must raise the money it needs by increasing federal taxes. Until we know which taxes will be increased we cannot say who will pay for the security given by the Act.

Much the same is true of the share in the cost to be paid by the state and local governments. Each authority has its own way of raising revenue. If the money is raised by a sales tax,

the cost will fall upon the consumers inside the
state who will, to a large extent, be wage-earners.
If it is raised by a poll tax, each person will have
to contribute the same amount of money whether
he is rich or poor. If a gasoline tax is levied to
raise funds, the cost of providing security will
fall upon the owners of automobiles, many of
whom are in the lower income brackets. These
are only some of the many ways in which the
states might raise money. Until we know the
exact method to be adopted, we cannot say who
will bear that part of the cost of economic
security which according to the Act is to be
provided out of state or local funds.

Summary

The difficulty of deciding who is to pay for
economic security has left its mark on the Social
Security Act. The Act appears at first to be a
great advance upon the haphazard way in which
we have distributed the costs of security in the
past. Yet the methods which it substitutes are in
turn unsatisfactory. The self-sustaining insurance
method of providing the funds for unemployment
compensation and old-age annuities has serious
disadvantages. Perhaps the greatest of these is
that it encourages evasion of the central and
difficult problem of cost distribution. The super-
ficial advantages of financing security in this

way are so beguiling that we overlook the fact that it also compels the poorer members of society to pay for their own security. Where in the financing of the unearned annuities the Act departs from the self-sustaining principle it does so in a peculiarly mean and unsatisfactory manner. The Act places upon the shoulders of workers who are now young the burden arising from our failure to set up an annuity plan many years ago, instead of calling upon those who are better able to pay, to share in the cost.

Collection of the money for social security solely out of taxes on employers and workers is open to other objections. It limits the security given and we must therefore devise other methods of taking care of the people altogether cut off from social insurance benefits and of those able to pay for only a small amount of security. To make the cost bearable, we build up a gargantuan savings fund or reserve, whose sole function is to yield interest but which will involve us in political and economic troubles.

It does not follow that no part of the money to finance economic security should be raised from taxes on employers and workers. Much can be said in favor of collecting some of the money in this way. But beyond a certain point taxes on employers have undesirable economic consequences and taxes on workers become an intolerable burden on an already low standard of living. This point may be reached before enough money has been obtained to provide adequate security. The solution is not to stop short of full security but to provide the additional funds necessary out of general taxation. The government should share the cost of unemployment benefits and old-age annuities with workers and employers. It could either contribute a certain sum each year or wait until employers' and workers' contributions fail to cover expenses and then make up the difference. The first method has been adopted in many European social insurance plans; the second was embodied in the original annuities plan of the Social Security Bill but was dropped in favor of the self-sustaining principle. We should do well to restore it.

The problem of proper financing is not solved even by a decision that at least some of the money shall be provided by general taxation. The kinds of taxes levied by the federal and state governments will determine who finally pays for economic security. Unless taxes are carefully selected the poor may still be compelled by a roundabout method to pay for their own security. It will be possible for the federal government for many years to obtain a great deal of the money needed to finance its share of the cost of security from the taxes paid by employers and workers for old-age annuities and unemployment compensation. If the burden is to fall on the strongest shoulders instead of the weakest the extra money needed must be raised from taxes falling on the relatively rich. The most certain way of shifting the burden in this direction is to raise the money by more steeply graduated inheritance and income taxes.

Chapter Ten

ECONOMIC SECURITY OR STATES RIGHTS

THE difficulties so far discussed must be faced by any capitalistic country providing economic security. There is an added problem in the United States: there are 48 state governments. These states, aware of their individuality and jealous of their independence, resist federal intervention in what they regard as their proper sphere. They have their special problems and their own ideas as to the proper way of solving them. The economic problems of the agricultural states are different from those of the industrial. The states whose employers engage largely in foreign trade have economic interests that differ from those whose economic life is more closely bound up with the home market. The southern states, in which colored people are important in numbers, have social problems not shared by the northern states.

Yet the states are not entirely independent. In spite of their political and social diversity they

177

form an indivisible economic whole. The prosperity of each is closely bound up with that of all the others. Changes in tastes and fashion in some states react seriously upon others. A general depression compelling Americans all over the country to stop buying automobiles means misery and depression concentrated in Detroit. Declining prosperity among farmers spells shrinking markets for goods manufactured in the industrial areas. The economic interdependence of the states is equally evident during periods of prosperity. America is a great free trade area. Goods move between one state and another, and to an employer in any one state the employers in all others are competitive rivals. Since there are no state immigration laws workers move freely about the country.

The Need for Uniformity of Protection

This diversity of social standards and economic interests in the different states, coupled with an underlying economic interdependence, increases the difficulties of providing economic security through governmental action. Just because the states have such different problems and varied ideas as to how to tackle them it is doubtful whether a uniform minimum of security for all Americans will ever be achieved if everything is left to the action of the states. Yet such a uniform minimum is desirable for both social and economic reasons.

No one denies that all Americans are entitled to a minimum of security against foreign attack. In emergencies we recognize by our actions, if not by our words, the rights of our fellow countrymen to an assurance of the bare necessities of life. A flood in the Mississippi Valley, an earthquake in California, a drought in the West, or a hurricane in Florida at once call forth offers of assistance from all parts of the country. National organizations like the Red Cross assist the stricken districts. We regard it as quite natural that the federal government should aid through sending the militia and in every other possible way. We have been slow to recognize that old age, unemployment, or sickness threaten existence as surely as the more spectacular "acts of God." The severity of the post-1930 depression compelled us to face realities and few people today would question the propriety of the use of federal money for relief purposes. If national responsibility for protecting the individual against physical hazards is accepted, the responsibility for securing him against the consequences of economic hazards can scarcely be rejected. There is no real difference between these two threats to security.

Even if uniform minimum guarantees are not urged for moral reasons, they are desirable on economic grounds. If workers can obtain in some states a security denied to them in others they will take this into account in deciding where to live and work. Differences in provision for the unemployed will considerably influence them. The man who works in New York and is entitled, when he is out of a job, to unemployment compensation as a right for a number of weeks will be unwilling, when unemployed, to accept work in neighboring parts of New Jersey or Connecticut. So long as these states pass no unemployment compensation laws he will reduce his chances of claiming unemployment benefits in the future by working within their borders. The provision of health insurance in some states and not in others would operate in the same way. However, as workers probably fear unemployment more than sickness, provision of unemployment benefits will attract workers and hold them in a state more than health insurance. But the latter will not be disregarded. If our much prized free flow of workers from one state to another is to be preserved, a uniform minimum of protection against economic insecurity is essential.

Such a uniform minimum could be obtained by placing the duty of providing security in the hands of the federal government. But apart from the unwillingness of the states to permit the federal government to exercise so much power, and the obvious federal unpreparedness for such work, this simple solution has one further disadvantage. It would abolish at a stroke the opportunities for experimentation in methods of providing security presented by the existence of 48 independent states.

The Value of Experimentation

The 48 states have rightly been called 48 laboratories. It is often said that this opportunity to explore new methods of solving social problems is one of the greatest advantages of the federal form of government, but this view is mistaken. Just because local conditions differ so greatly a method that has proved successful in one state may be unsuitable in others. It is of course easier to experiment on a small scale. Once the objective is agreed upon, it is desirable that the methods of achieving it should so far as possible be suited to the special conditions of each state. But we should be blinding our eyes to realities if we failed to recognize that unlimited freedom of the states to experiment without federal intervention of any kind must seriously limit the security provided.

In the first place, freedom to experiment means both freedom not to experiment and freedom to prove again, and at heavy cost, what is already known—that there are some methods that will not work. The social standards and ideals of the states vary widely and the value they place upon economic security differs. If the provision of economic security is to be handed over to the states, many will not experiment at all. There are still four states which have failed to enact even the most simple and basic laws governing hours of employment for women. Four states still have no workmen's compensation laws, although the first acts were passed as long ago as 1911. We can count on our fingers the number of states that have set up unemployment compensation plans. The plea for the opportunity to experiment is almost invariably illustrated by the citation of the achievements of a small handful of progressive states, which like a stage army, do duty again and again. The much larger number of states which have taken little or no advantage of their unlimited opportunity to experiment in providing economic security is often forgotten. Past history plainly shows that if we rely on state action alone many millions of workers will obtain no economic security. We must choose between experimentation and security. A large part of the failure of the Social Security Act to provide full security is due to the way in which the framers of the Act have made this fundamental choice.

The Act, in the main, has preferred state autonomy and the right to experiment to the assurance of a uniform minimum of security. Except in the provision of old-age annuities and the small sum to be spent by the United States Public Health Office, the decision whether there is to be security or not is left to the individual states.

The Necessity for Federal Participation

State experimentation without federal assistance is unlikely to provide a uniform minimum security for another reason. Some kinds of experiments can never be carried very far by the states without help from the federal government. The selected method of financing may cause the difficulty. If a state desires to experiment with taxes on payrolls its employers can very properly argue that they will be placed at a disadvantage as compared with their competitors in other states which do not finance economic security in this way. Thus one state can experiment along these lines only if it knows that others will follow suit immediately or after not too long an interval. The federal payroll taxes in the unemployment compensation program are, as we have seen, aimed to remove this difficulty. Without some device of this kind carried through by the federal government, it is difficult to see how any experiment that involves taxing producers can be carried through on a state basis.

The desire of the states to experiment in the provision of economic security may also be thwarted because of the probable cost, which varies greatly from state to state. The Committee on Economic Security reported that in the years 1930–1933 the percentage of unemployment in the different states varied all the way from 34.3 per cent in Michigan to 17 per cent in Georgia. Thus the least fortunate state had just twice as much unemployment as the most fortunate. In April, 1930, when the depression was beginning and 8.5 per cent of our wage earners were unemployed in the country as a whole, the percentage in Michigan was 13.9 per cent or 63.5 per cent above the national average; it was more than three times as great as that of South Dakota, where the percentage was 3.9 per cent.

The burden carried by the various states varies also in other fields of insecurity. Old people prefer to live in the more pleasant and less extreme climates. Consequently, sooner or later we should expect the proportion of the aged in the population to be especially high in states like

Florida and California. Young workers tend to go where there are opportunities for work, returning when they are old to the farms or the parts of the country from which they originally came. It is hardly surprising that the proportion of old people in the total population in such states as Michigan (5.3 per cent) and Illinois (5.5 per cent) is less than that in New Hampshire (8.9 per cent) or Vermont (8.7 per cent) which traditionally send their sons to work in other parts of the country. Pensions to the aged will therefore be a heavier burden in some states than in others.

The states differ also in the extent of their health bills. Those with a relatively large number of poorer people are particularly susceptible to certain kinds of diseases. Their children are more apt to die when infants because they cannot get the proper care, and the death rate among mothers is also high. In Arizona and New Mexico more than 90 babies died out of every thousand born alive in 1933. At the same time the infant death rate for the country as a whole was only 58. In the same year, in the country as a whole, 62 mothers out of every 10,000 died in pregnancy or childbirth, but in Florida the number was 115 and in New Mexico 86, while in Idaho it was only 43 and in Minnesota 44. For several reasons these death rates are higher among the colored population. During

1933, 91 colored babies out of every thousand born alive died in the first year of life as compared with 53 white babies. Efforts to reduce this high death rate will be especially costly in states where the colored population is large.

Experimentation is therefore a costly privilege. The stern moralist may say that the cost is the necessary price of independence. The economic realist may reply that the shift of the cotton industry to the South brings lower prices to all cotton users but concentrates the costs of the change in New England; some share in maintaining the New England unemployed should, therefore, be carried by consumers in other states. Each person must decide for himself whether or not the states *ought* to bear the full costs of their own experiments in providing security.

In any event it is a cold fact that if they are compelled to do so many people will obtain no economic security. The need for security is often greatest in precisely those areas where there is most poverty and depression, and, therefore, least ability to pay. Thus the federal government must somewhat equalize the burden between different states if there is to be any complete program. It has done so in the pension plans for the aged, for dependent children, and for the blind, and through the appropriation to assist states in administering unemployment compensation laws. The grants to encourage the development of maternal and child welfare services and to improve the health of special classes of people, or of the community in general, have the same objective. But only in making these latter grants and those for unemployment compensation does the federal government recognize the greater need of the especially poverty-stricken areas or those whose costs are higher. The offer to share in the cost of pensions is made equally to all states regardless of their economic standing.

Finally, some experiments in the provision of economic security can never be carried out by individual states. We have seen that some public health experiments can be conducted only by the federal government. Certain experiments aimed at stabilizing employment cannot be effective on a state basis. Employment can often be regularized only by action undertaken by a whole industry. Efforts made by the members of an industry only in states having unemployment compensation laws will be thwarted by the action of rivals in states exercising no pressure to regularize production. The large concern which has branches in many states can often stabilize employment only by treating the whole enterprise as a unit and shifting orders, if not workers, from one plant to another. Such operations will be particularly difficult if the stabilization plans have to conform to the requirements of a number of state laws.

Experiments in some methods of providing old-age security are impossible on any but a federal basis. This is the case with a contributory old-age annuities plan. The young worker who must pay taxes for many years wants to be assured that by the time he is old he will obtain an annuity. But he also wants to be free to move about the country at will. If he works in different states during 45 years of his working life, his chances of accumulating an adequate annuity will depend on the existence of an annuity law in each state. He cannot spend his old age in the more pleasant climates of Florida or California if we have only state systems, and California and Florida happen to decide not to provide old-age annuities. On the other hand, the federal government can scarcely guarantee this man's annuity if all the states are free at any time to decide whether or not they will support the system. It might find itself committed to pay tremendous sums to the workers who had made contributions in good faith when they were young. But if the states had by then decided to stop collecting contributions, it would have no income with which to pay the annuities as they fell due.

If security in old age is to take the form of annuities provided out of payments collected over a long period of years, while workers are to be free to move from one state to another, a federal system is inevitable. In recognition of these facts the Social Security Act provides for a federal old-age annuities plan.

Summary

The provision of economic security through governmental action faces peculiar problems in the United States where the business of government is shared between federal and state authorities. Although politically independent, the states are economically interdependent and have widely differing social ideals. No uniform measure of minimum security can therefore be attained if states are left to experiment at will. Some states will provide no security; others will be restricted in their activity by the fear of interstate competition or of the costs involved. Some ways of providing security can be carried through only by a super-state authority. A certain measure of federal participation is essential.

The Social Security Act recognizes these difficulties by providing for so-called federal-state cooperation in all parts of the program except the old-age annuities and certain public health services where the federal government is the sole authority. Is this division of authority a good one? Has federal-state cooperation been extended into fields in which adequate security can be provided only by a federal plan?

Where federal-state cooperation is relied upon, the federal government confines itself to an effort to remove obstacles to state action, an offer to share in the cost of security programs, and a rather feeble attempt to raise the standards of the security provided. Thus the main responsibility and initiative lie in the hands of the states. How much supervision and control should there be in return for federal assistance? Is the variation in the conditions to be satisfied by the states in different parts of the program essential or desirable? How far will the conditions insisted upon ensure a reasonable minimum of economic security? How far are the devices adopted by the Act likely to be effective in achieving their objective? These are the questions we must deal with in the following chapter.

Chapter Eleven

THE ADMINISTRATION OF ECONOMIC SECURITY

Is the federal government especially suited to administer some kinds of security and the states to administer others? The great variety in the nature of the security provided and the methods of financing adopted preclude a simple answer. There is no single rule by which we can judge. We cannot even say that the states are the ideal areas for reasons of size alone. If Delaware or Rhode Island are the right size for economical administration of an unemployment compensation plan or an old-age pension system, then Texas cannot be. The populations in the states vary in size as much as do their areas. We can reach a decision only by looking at each part of the security program and asking what problems it presents.

Old-age Annuities

We have already seen that the very nature of an old-age annuities scheme in a country in which workers move from state to state calls for a super-state plan. The administrative problems involved point in the same direction. Administration of such a plan is relatively simple. The federal government has tax officers in every state who can collect the contributions from employers and workers. It is true that it will be necessary to keep records of the wages received by workers throughout their working lives so long as the amount of the annuity is based upon past earnings. But as workers move about the country these records can be kept most simply by one rather than by 48 authorities. No needs test is applied to those who claim annuities. They have to prove only that they have paid a certain number of contributions (which can be verified from the tax records) and that they are sixty-five years of age (usually not very difficult to establish). The annuity can be paid through post office checks mailed every month to the annuitants. And this also the federal government can conveniently do. The tremendous funds that will accumulate probably can be invested more safely and economically by a single federal authority than by 48 separate authorities. It is also easier to see what is happening to them when they are gathered together in the hands of one authority. Complete federal administration of the annuity plan is overwhelmingly indicated and in this respect the Social Security Act is well devised.

Old-age Pensions

Old-age assistance pensions present somewhat different problems. Every pensioner must prove that he is in need. Since the states and their local authorities have for many years been investigating need, it may be argued that they should take charge of this part of the work in order to secure the benefit of their special experience. On the other hand, if it is desired to make a sharp distinction between old-age pensions and other kinds of public assistance, it may not be desirable to place the work of investigation in the hands of the usual public welfare investigators. The officials used could be controlled either by the federal or the state authorities. The machinery built up under the Federal Emergency Relief Administration provides a foundation for federally controlled investigation. But the Relief Administration has been compelled to enlist the cooperation of local people, and the search for a definition of need that would apply to all parts of the country has not been very successful. Since local standards must necessarily play a large part in defining need, there are good reasons for leaving this work to state authorities, even though the work be separated from the administration of the public welfare system.

There are other reasons for leaving the greater part of the administration of old-age pensions to the states. We have seen that the Act does not bluntly say that the pensions must provide any given standard of living, but they are obviously intended to enable old people to maintain themselves in decency and health. Since economic conditions and social standards vary so greatly, this phrase will be interpreted very differently in different states. In a farming district old people may need less cash than in a built-up city area where rents are higher and there is no chance for a small garden or cheap fuel. Each state will realize more clearly and directly than would a central authority the consequences of interpreting the phrase narrowly or generously. The Social Security Act probably follows a wise course, therefore, in leaving the administration of the pensions plan in the hands of the states. But it is unfortunate that the Act did not require the payment of pensions sufficient to provide a minimum of health and decency. Each state would have been free to interpret that phrase as it wished, but it could have been called upon to justify its interpretation to the Social Security Board. The aged might thus have been protected from the worst kinds of shabby economy.

Unemployment Compensation and Unemployment Relief

The administration of unemployment compensation presents greater difficulties. Consequently there is a sharp difference of opinion between those who desire a federal and those who desire a state plan. The choice is, however, less difficult than it seems at first sight. It must never be forgotten that there are likely always to be at least two methods of giving security against unemployment. Even if all 48 states immediately set up unemployment compensation plans conforming to the standards of the Social Security Act, they would cover little more than one-third of the wage earners of the country. With the revival of trade 60 per cent of the wage earners might be covered. But the benefits will be given only for about 12 or 15 weeks. We saw in Chapter Eight that it would be undesirable to extend this period indefinitely even though it might with advantage be longer than the present limit. Thus there will still be thousands of unemployed people, even in normal times, whose need for security will not be satisfied. When trade is bad this group will certainly be much larger than that taken care of by state compensation plans and may well reach into the millions. Some other way must be found of providing for these people. If then there will always be at least two ways of dealing with the unemployed, should one or both be entrusted to the states or to the federal government? Or should both be administered on a federal-state basis?

The unemployment compensation plans have been described as a "first line of defense" against loss of income. At first sight it seems that this "first line of defense" should be federally administered. In normal times it will meet the needs of the greater number of unemployed workers, especially if the duration of benefit is extended beyond the present limits. We have already seen that a minimum uniformity of protection is essential if the free movement of workers from state to state is not to be checked. Under a federal plan the rights of workers moving from state to state could be protected more simply. No worker would have his benefits curtailed because he happened to live in a state where unemployment was unusually heavy. No worker would be penalized because his state failed to pass the necessary laws.

The alternative solution involving state plans meeting minimum standards prescribed by the federal government would be more clumsy even if all states passed laws. It would call for agreements between all the different states to recognize claims based on employment outside their own borders. A vast reinsurance plan would be necessary to equalize the burden between states.

The payment of unemployment compensation has, as we saw in Chapter Eight, direct effects upon the rise and fall of wages. A nation incurs an economic risk when it makes such payments, namely the risk of resisting deliberately the tendency for wages to fall when unemployment is widespread and workers must choose between lower wages and no income at all. By shortening or lengthening the period for which unemployment benefits are paid unaccompanied by pressure to take work at less than prevailing wages, the risk is reduced or increased.

The question whether pressure should be applied to reduce rates of wages, in the hope of reviving business, concerns the country as a whole. It is not always easy to know whether a revival would be brought about by reducing money wages without taking account of business conditions in all parts of the country. The decision cannot be properly made by the individual states, which are inevitably influenced by local rather than national conditions. Only some central super-state authority is in a position to weigh the varying interests of the different parts of the country and to have access to the relevant information on which a judgment must be based. Power to raise or lower the general rate of interest throughout the country is already centralized (in the Federal Reserve Board). Why not centralize also the power to make decisions affecting the general level of wages?

The case in favor of a federal first line of defense against unemployment is strengthened by the fact that unemployment compensation is much simpler to administer than other ways of dealing with unemployment. The administrators have to exercise little or no discretion and do not need any special knowledge of local conditions and standards. One of the most difficult problems of a purely relief program, namely, the determination of the amount of the benefit, does not arise. All the existing American plans fix the benefits as a percentage of previous wages. Thus in those parts of the country where wages are low benefits will automatically be low, and in the high wage districts benefits will be high. There will be no danger that the federal government would fix benefits dangerously nearer to local wage levels in some parts of the country than in others.

Unemployment compensation also differs from relief in requiring no test of need. The arguments in favor of a state-administered pension plan, therefore, do not apply to unemployment compensation. Local knowledge of standards of living and of the private resources of claimants is not required. Workers who claim benefits must prove only that they have been insured for the necessary number of weeks, and that they are willing to work, and capable of work, but unable to get a job. It would be quite easy under a federal plan to verify a worker's claim to have been insured. Indeed, provision could much more easily be made for the needs of workers who work now in one state, now in another. Under a federal plan it would be necessary to consult only one instead of 49 sets of records.

In order to test whether workers are genuinely willing to work but unable to obtain employment, it will of course be necessary to set up employment offices which are in a position to know whether jobs are available and to offer them to workers. Here again a chain of offices operated by the federal government would probably be more satisfactory than separate offices operated by the various states. Experience under the Wagner-Peyser Act, whereby the federal government tries to cooperate with the states in setting up such offices, has already demonstrated the difficulties of building up a satisfactory chain of employment bureaus when the initiative is left in the hands of the states. But even if satisfactory employment offices were set up by every state in the Union, it would still, under state schemes, be necessary to arrange for the interchange of information. There may often be a shortage of workers in one state while there is unemployment in another. Without a central clearing house of information many workers will not be placed in jobs even though there are openings for them.

The unemployment compensation method of providing security also has the advantage that it simplifies the selection of those entitled to compensation. It is always difficult to decide what kinds of work people may refuse without losing the right to benefits. It is impossible to refuse all benefits if they reject any job regardless of the rate of pay, kind of work, or location of the job. But it is difficult to draw a line between suitable and unsuitable offers of work. Unemployment compensation differs from other less pleasant forms of relief in that, for the limited time for which compensation is paid, workers are permitted to refuse jobs at substantially less than prevailing wages, and often also in distant places, or in unfamiliar occupations without losing their right to benefit.

Thus both in the interests of uniformity of protection and because it is the easier of the

two systems to administer, there is a great deal
to be said for making unemployment compensation a federal or national plan. By the same token
the second line of defense, because it calls for the
making of difficult decisions about individual
cases and for adjustment to local conditions, can
more conveniently be administered by the states
or smaller local authorities. The federal government, because of its greater financial resources
and borrowing powers, will probably have to give
financial assistance. It might use the grant-in-aid
method, as in the old-age pensions plan. But once
it is decided that pressure should be applied to
reduce wages, there is a good deal to be said for
letting each state decide how much pressure to
apply and how to apply it. The decision to deny
benefits because workers have refused jobs at
less than going wages makes the task of administering unemployment relief vastly more difficult.
It calls for the exercise of discretion. It is necessary to know a great deal about local conditions
and about the kinds of work performed in the
district. Decisions concerning the suitability of
specific jobs for specific workers could scarcely
be made by a central authority.

It is probable that the second line of defense
against unemployment will restrict benefits to
people who are in need. We have already seen
that there are many reasons why the carrying

through of a security program involving in-
vestigations into need should be left in the hands
of the states. Finally, many of the people to be
cared for by the second line of defense will be
workers who have been unemployed so long that
they can no longer claim unemployment compensation benefits. If work relief is to play a part
in the program, it should be provided first of all
for those workers who have been longest unemployed, for their morale will be at the lowest ebb.
Giving security by creating jobs, whether in the
form of public works or work relief, raises many
new problems. The government must decide
what level of wages can be paid on these projects
without unfairness to workers who are in private
employment. It must decide what kinds of
projects are most needed and will interfere least
with private business. And the possibilities of
development of the area and the skills of the
local unemployed must both be taken into
account. Such decisions can best be made locally
by people informed about local conditions. Here
is a field in which there is great scope for the
inventiveness and ingenuity of the different
states.

Consideration of the problems involved in
giving security to all the unemployed and not
merely to a section of them suggests, therefore,
that there is a good case for handing over the

administration of the much simpler first line of defense to the federal government. While the latter may have to put up some of the money to assist those who get no security under the unemployment compensation plans, it seems desirable to leave this second line of defense very largely to the states. In their hands should lie the responsibility for working out plans, for deciding what test of need shall be applied, what degree of pressure shall be put on local people to compel them to accept jobs, what kinds of jobs are suitable to each worker in the circumstances, and what kinds of work projects shall be undertaken.

Unfortunately it would be foolish to pretend that the federal government is at present in a position to carry out even the relatively simple tasks in connection with the payment of cash or compensation benefits. The task is simple only in comparison with that of dealing with the long-period unemployed, of finding suitable jobs and projects for them, and of deciding how much pressure to apply. It is still a tremendous undertaking. The federal government has almost no experience in this field and is not beyond criticism in its appointment of officials to carry out the functions which it already has to perform, even though it has accepted civil service standards to a greater degree than many of the states. Undoubtedly several years will be needed to solve all the problems connected with this new kind of governmental activity. For this reason many people who believe that an unemployment compensation plan administered by the federal government would be preferable to one controlled by the states also believe that the time is not yet ripe for such a development. We are paying the price of inexperience.

The best solution, from the administrative point of view alone, would probably be to set up, to begin with, an unemployment compensation plan developed on a state basis but meeting federal minimum standards and designed so that it could easily be converted into a national plan when the federal administrative machinery has been developed and improved. The Act does indeed provide for state unemployment compensation plans. But while making state action possible the federal government does not in return require that the state plans must meet essential basic standards. Moreover, as we shall see below, the manner of the provision will make later transformation into a federal plan very difficult.

The Health Program

Whether the plan for providing security against the hazards of ill health should be a federal or a local one will depend upon the kinds of benefits we try to give. If we limit ourselves to encouraging research and general public health work it seems probable that the division of responsibility will be determined fairly easily by the nature of the problem to be tackled. If we attack sickness by picking out some groups of people and helping them rather than others because they are needy, there is no reason why we should not continue with the state plan provided for in the Act.

The proper allocation of responsibility becomes more difficult if we decide that in addition we want to use some form of social insurance to protect the average man or woman from the burden of sickness bills and the loss of income due to permanent or temporary disability. These two hazards call for different treatment, and raise, therefore, different problems. Most countries have found it advantageous to separate the administration of cash benefits from the administration of curative services. If loss of earning power is to be compensated by a cash payment many of the problems will be similar to those met with in unemployment compensation, and the consequences of not giving equal protection against loss of income will be similar. The case in favor of an ultimate federal plan is very strong, even though, as with unemployment compensation, it may be deemed wise to begin

205

with a federal-state plan. The payment of a specified percentage of previous earnings in return for contributions made in the past would solve the problem of the amount of benefit to be paid in different parts of the country. The main difficulty would center around the determination of a man's claim to be "unfit for work." If, as was suggested in Chapter Five, the local attendant physician must certify his patients' condition, the board of medical referees to decide disputed cases might still be a federal or super-state body.

But the treatment of sickness raises different problems and calls for much closer cooperation with the medical profession at every stage, and for adaptation to local conditions. The medical facilities of the different states vary widely, and the local medical associations have their own traditions, types of organization, and relationships to their own local authorities. However desirable a minimum uniformity of treatment and medical care may be, it would be impossible at this stage to achieve this by a unified federal plan. More progress is likely to be achieved by permitting the states to make their own arrangements with the local medical associations. In such a program the federal government might play a part by offering financial assistance if the state plans conform to certain basic standards.

Security for Widows and Orphans

Whether the provision of security to dependents should be a state or federal function depends also on the kind of security finally selected. Security to widows and to children is provided under the Act only if they are in need and have no one who can support them. This kind of security is probably best provided by states, aided by federal encouragement in the form of financial help. But here too, the federal government should lay down minimum conditions in order to ensure that all dependents in the states claiming federal aid have equal chances of assistance and of assistance that is real. If ever we should decide to give to dependents security similar to that to be given in the future to older people under the annuities plan, it would probably be both simpler and more satisfactory to have a federal rather than a state system. If, for example, we provide survivors' pensions or larger death benefits, people will pay contributions for many years, and the federal government alone is in a position to guarantee workers the future benefits regardless of where they have worked and where they may reside at the time of death. Since there would be no test of need, the administrative work would be greatly simplified and would not be too much for the resources of the federal government.

Techniques of Federal-State Cooperation

The main responsibility for social security programs is likely to rest for many years in the hands of the states. The federal government will, however, participate by making it easy for the competing states to set up plans and by attempting to raise standards. In the Social Security Act the federal government uses two quite different methods of attaining these objectives. On the one hand, in the grants for administration of unemployment compensation and in the programs for pensions to the aged, the young, and the blind, and for the promotion of health, the federal government grants subsidies to the states if they meet certain conditions. On the other hand, in the unemployment compensation plan, the federal government levies a tax on employers throughout the country but allows them to deduct from this tax a large part of what they contribute toward approved state unemployment compensation plans. Why are two methods used to bring about the same result? Is one preferable to the other?

The usefulness of each of these devices depends to some extent upon the selected method of financing the security plan. If at least part of the money is to be raised by taxes on employers, then, as we saw on page 183, a federal tax on all those employers who do not pay to a state fund is inevitable to prevent penalization of employers paying the tax, as compared with their rivals in other states. This is why the unemployment compensation plan embodies the ingenious 3 per cent tax device whereas no such federal tax is necessary to the other parts of the security program in which both federal and state governments cooperate; the money is provided in another way.

The necessity for a federal tax on employers even though the compensation plans are to be on a state basis can thus be explained. But it is not so easy to account for the curious way in which the money is returned to the states. Why should the federal government not pay back the money it has collected, direct to the states in the form of grants or subsidies, just as it gives grants from federal funds in the old-age and blind pensions plans, and in the grants for dependent children? Why adopt the roundabout method (sometimes called the Wagner-Lewis plan) of giving it back to the states through a tax offset to each individual employer?

It cannot be because the offset method is easier to administer. On the contrary it is much more troublesome and complicated. Every em-

209

ployer in states establishing plans will pay two sets of taxes, make out two sets of returns, and be investigated by two sets of officials. This would be bad enough if the coverage of the federal and the state laws were identical. But, as we have seen, this is not the case. The workers in respect of whom an employer must pay the federal tax do not coincide with those for whom he must pay a state payroll tax. The federal law covers the total payroll whereas the state laws tax wages or salaries only up to $2,500 or $3,000. This duplication increases the costs of administration and is likely to prove extremely irritating to employers.

Collection of the funds by the federal government would make it easier to secure that all the money needed for the state unemployment compensation plans is deposited in the Unemployment Trust Fund as required in the Act. Under the present offset plan the money will be collected by the states, handed over to the federal government for safekeeping, and handed back again to the states when they make benefit payments, an unnecessary amount of transferring and account keeping.

Workers who move from state to state could much more easily be protected if state plans were financed by grants or subsidies from the federal government. The latter could offer to the states a grant to pay the benefits for workers who had worked only in that state, and it could keep back, from the money it had collected, sufficient funds to finance the benefits of those who had recently been employed in more than one state. It might even keep back some of the money to help those states in which unemployment was especially heavy. Under the present tax offset plan such arrangements can be made only by voluntary agreements among 49 authorities. Complete protection of the rights of workers would require 1225 agreements.

The grant-in-aid method of returning the money collected by the federal government to the states is much more effective than the tax offset method as a means of raising the standards of the state plans. Apart from the fact that the federal government could probably lay down more conditions under the grant-in-aid plan without running foul of the Supreme Court, it could also secure more effectively the fulfillment of those conditions. It could more easily refuse to make any grant to a state whose plan does not meet the federal requirements. Under the present tax offset arrangement, it must resort to the clumsy device of refusing to allow tax-paying employers to deduct their state contributions from the federal tax. Thousands of tax returns filled in by employers who do not understand what is happening must be sent back to them. Any attempt to use this power will probably make the federal government unpopular with employers who are unlikely to realize that the trouble lies with their own state government. The federal government will be unwilling to use this weapon if it can possibly avoid it. Financing by grant-in-aid allows the federal government to put direct pressure on the state governments. The tax offset method requires that pressure be applied through thousands of employers who at best will be put to a great deal of inconvenience, and who at worst will have to pay two taxes instead of one.

The grant-in-aid arrangement also has the great advantage that transference to a national unemployment compensation scheme can be more easily made. Its greater convenience and effectiveness would probably have brought about greater uniformity of protection than is likely to result from the tax offset. Thus the change would be less abrupt. Moreover, if they had never collected the payroll taxes the states would not feel that when the change was made they were handing over to the federal government a source of revenue that belonged properly to them.

Why then was the grant-in-aid method of federal-state cooperation not used in the unemployment compensation plan although adopted in every other part of the federal-state security program? It is an open secret that the less effective tax offset was favored in some quarters just because it obstructed federal efforts to secure uniform minimum standards. Those who treasured the rights of their states to experiment with devices for stabilizing employment were unwilling that the federal government should set standards which might prevent them from trying certain methods. To these people were added others who believed (erroneously, as we shall see in the following chapter) that in the event of the Security Act being held unconstitutional, state plans would be more likely to continue on an independent basis if built up under the tax offset method. Finally, there were some who believed a federal grant-in-aid to be too precarious a basis for security plans. If Congress failed to vote the money in any year the plan would fall to the ground. This danger is real, but as we shall see, not conclusive, especially when the number of voters affected by the legislation is very large.

Summary

If the administration of a security program must be shared between the federal and state governments, the proper sphere of activity of each must be carefully considered. The respec-

tive parts to be played by the federal and by the
state governments depend upon the kind of
decisions that have to be made and the kinds of
duties to be performed. These vary from plan
to plan in each of the four major fields of insecurity on account of the difference in the kind of
security provided and the selected methods of
financing.

The old-age annuities plan raises no serious
problems. The method of financing allows a
choice only between a federal plan or none at all.
The administrative work involved will also be
relatively simple and of a type that the federal
government is equipped to handle. The old-age
pension plan, while calling for federal financial
aid, involves administrative work such as the
investigation of need and the determination of
standards of living that can more suitably be
performed by the states or their local authorities.
By the same token pensions to widows and
orphans and to the blind, so long as they are
conditional upon proof of need, should be administered by the states. The federal government
should, however, in return for its financial
assistance, require the states in all pension
plans to provide at least a respectable minimum
of security.

Unemployment presents greater difficulties.
Only a federal plan can provide a uniform mini-

mum of protection without an intolerably complex administrative system. Yet at some stage it may become desirable to apply pressure to the unemployed to take unfamiliar jobs, or jobs at less than prevailing wages, or to pay unemployment benefits only on proof of need, or to give assistance in the form of the offer of a job instead of the payment of a cash income. These matters are all more suitable for administration by the states and local authorities than by a federal authority. They require the exercise of discretion and an intimate knowledge of local problems and needs. A compromise between federal and state administration in any complete unemployment security program is therefore indicated.

Two distinct systems of unemployment assistance are probably necessary. The first, or unemployment compensation system, would provide benefits for a limited period, based upon past earnings and paid regardless of need and without any pressure on workers to accept jobs at less than prevailing rates. This first line of defense should be administered on a federal basis. It involves less complicated administrative work and would, in normal times, secure a uniform minimum of protection regardless of place of residence or employment to the great majority of the unemployed. The second line of defense

215

involves tests of need, pressure to take work, and the development of work relief programs to be administered by the states, although part of the money would be supplied by the federal government, perhaps in the form of a grant-in-aid.

Since the federal government is none too well equipped at present to handle even the simpler first line of defense, a further compromise may be necessary. State plans should be developed meeting minimum federal standards and capable of easy transformation into a national plan. The tax offset method of financing, adopted in the Security Act, will, however, hinder such a transformation.

Security against the hazards of health must take at least two forms: provision of income to those prevented from working, and treatment for those who are sick. If social insurance is used to achieve these objectives, the plan for providing income should probably be administered ultimately by the federal government, while that providing treatment should be administered by the states.

The Social Security Act fails to ensure adequate federal participation in the total security program. The federal government contributes a large proportion of the cost of the old-age pensions, mothers' pensions, and blind pensions. But it fails to lay down, as a condition of its assistance, effective minimum standards of security. In the unemployment compensation plan it undertakes vast new responsibilities to enable the states to provide unemployment compensation financed by taxes on employers, but fails to require in return the payment of at least a minimum unemployment benefit for a specified period. It shares in the costs of administration of many of the state programs but has been denied the right to insist on civil service standards in the appointment of officials in charge of the work.

Fear of undermining the independence and vigor of the states explains many of these vital omissions. The maintenance of States' Rights may, of course, be preferred to the provision of more complete security. But if so, it must be recognized that state independence is being upheld at the expense of the insecure.

Chapter Twelve

IS SOCIAL SECURITY
CONSTITUTIONAL?

IT is often said that there are not 49 but 50 governments in the United States, and that the fiftieth, which is the Supreme Court, is the most powerful of them all for it is able to undo the work of all the others. Every law must, if challenged, pass the test of constitutionality, and the Supreme Court is the final judge. In the last few years a number of important pieces of legislation have disappeared from the scene because they have been challenged in this way and the governments concerned have failed to satisfy the Supreme Court.

The Constitutional Vulnerability of the Act

The Social Security Act may in its turn meet this test. The federal government must show that the provisions of the challenged law do not exceed the powers permitted to it under the Constitution. It is the more likely to be challenged because the federal government is trying some new experiments. Many people dislike experimentation of this kind and will argue that the government has exceeded its constitutional powers.

The powers of the federal government cannot be discovered merely by looking at the dry language of the Constitution. Chief Justice Hughes once pointed out that "we are under a constitution but the Constitution is what the judges say it is." By their power to interpret, the judges have molded the Constitution to what they believe to be the developing needs of the country. It is to the interpretations which they have made that we must look for an understanding of the words written in the Constitution.

Nothing in the Constitution expressly forbids the federal government to legislate for social security. On the other hand, the federal government possesses only such powers as have been conferred upon it, and there are admittedly no words in the Constitution expressly conferring upon it the power to enact a social security program of the kind we have been discussing. The problem of social security was not in the minds of the founders of the Constitution. They could not have thought in these terms, for social insurance or similar programs did not then exist.

219

But many acts have been held to be within the power of Congress because they could be inferred from other powers expressly given. The immediate question is, therefore, whether the Constitution can and will be molded so as to bring the furtherance of such a program within the powers of the federal government as defined.

Under the Social Security Act the federal government seeks to exercise its powers in three distinct ways, each of which may be challenged. It undertakes to give money to the states to assist them to carry through certain programs. It makes use of the taxing power to raise money for old-age annuities. And it also employs this same taxing power to encourage the states to set up unemployment compensation programs.

The first question concerns the power of the federal government to grant money to a state for expenditure on projects upon which the federal government itself could not spend directly. The Court has never yet stated that it would hold such action improper. The fact that the federal government has been permitted to grant money in this way in the past (for education, child welfare, and other purposes) strengthens the probability that it will be upheld in the present instance.

One of the powers given to Congress is the power to levy taxes to provide for the general welfare. The old-age annuities plan will ultimately involve the question whether the federal government can defend the use of its constitutional power to tax, for the purpose of raising funds for old-age annuities, on the ground that it is providing for the general welfare by doing so. The answer depends upon the meaning given to the words "general welfare" by the Supreme Court, which has not yet precisely defined them.

The unemployment compensation features of the Act present a somewhat different problem. Here the Act creates no federal system but merely seeks to induce the states to set up plans of their own. The tax offset method has been approved before, in at least one instance. But it remains for the Court to decide whether the levy on employers of eight or more workers is a true tax or a penalty whereby Congress seeks indirectly to regulate where it has no direct power. If it is held to be the latter, it will be declared unconstitutional, as was the somewhat similar child labor tax in 1922. The recent A.A.A. decision makes it still more doubtful whether the Court will regard the unemployment compensation tax as a true tax.

The fear of constitutional challenge has left its mark on the Security Act in only one important respect. Except for the sections relating to unemployment compensation, Congress has

not allowed consideration of the probable out-
come of a constitutional challenge materially to
influence its choice of methods of providing
security. Fear of an unfavorable decision from
the Supreme Court was, however, in considerable
measure responsible for the adoption in the unemployment compensation plan of the tax offset
instead of the grant-in-aid as a way of returning
to the states the taxes collected from their
employers. It was believed that since the tax
offset method required the states not only to
pass their own laws but also to collect the taxes
themselves, these laws might remain in existence
even if the Social Security Act was declared
unconstitutional. If the federal government alone
collected the money and paid it back to the
states as a 100 per cent subsidy, it was feared
that the lapse of the Social Security Act would
bring all state unemployment schemes to an end.
This argument is not very sound. In so far as the
states set up compensation plans only because
the federal government is taxing their employers
3 per cent of payrolls, they are unlikely to continue their acts if the federal tax disappears.
Indeed, many of the states have foreseen this
possibility and have provided either that their
own acts shall remain in effect only so long as the
federal Act continues, or that the tax imposed
shall be equal to 90 per cent of the tax collected

by the federal government. If the federal tax is no longer levied, the state tax will also cease.

Amendment of the Law

If the Supreme Court disapproves of the methods selected by Congress in the Social Security Act, must we despair of ever obtaining economic security with the aid or participation of the federal government? Such a pessimistic conclusion seems hardly justified. To begin with, the pitfalls before the Security Act concern different parts of the total program. The most vulnerable sections are probably those relating to the unemployment compensation and contributory old-age annuities plans. The various pension plans and the grants for health services involving merely an offer of money to the states, without compulsion upon them to do anything, are in line with accepted practice which the courts have never yet interfered with, and may well be held constitutional. The Act contains a clause stating that each part stands by itself. Thus even if some of the features are declared unconstitutional others may survive.

Some of the difficulties might perhaps be avoided by changing the method of financing economic security. If the Court approves of the grants-in-aid features of the Act but decides that the federal government may not impose a tax in order to finance old-age annuity benefits, or to stimulate the states to set up unemployment compensation plans, it might still be possible to provide these same benefits but to finance them out of general federal taxation. The federal government could then either set up a scale of benefits itself, or leave the states to do so and furnish them with the necessary funds.

This way of financing security benefits is open to many objections. The federal government could, it is true, grant money to the states or to individuals subject to such conditions as it wished. But if the benefits are not directly related to the amount of money that must be raised to pay for them, there is a real danger that the federal government will continually be pressed to be more and more generous at the public expense. The fight over the veterans' bonus and the power of the veterans' lobby have revealed the consequences of pressure by determined groups for more and more benefits, which must come out of general taxation. No group finds it worth while to oppose the extension of these benefits. Each individual hopes that the other fellow will pay and forgets how the bill for the pork barrel is mounting. One of the great advantages of the social insurance way of determining the level of benefits lies in the fact that a considerable part of the cost is paid by workers and employers who will directly feel the increased financial burden of increased benefits.

There is also another objection to the attempt to surmount the constitutional difficulty by providing the money for economic security out of general federal taxation. If no funds are earmarked for this purpose the continuance of the whole plan depends upon the willingness of Congress to grant money from year to year. If no money is voted no payments can be made. The Social Security Act experienced this difficulty almost as soon as it was passed. Owing to a last minute Congressional tangle at the end of the 1935 session, no appropriations were made for the parts of the security program financed by federal grants. In consequence the aged, the young, and the blind had to wait another year for their security. Those states which have passed unemployment compensation laws relying on federal grants to cover the costs of administration find themselves committed to a program with little or no means of putting it into effect.

The earlier program for child and maternal welfare, the money for which was voted in the original Sheppard-Towner Act only for a limited period, was also brought to a sudden end by the failure of Congress to vote any further funds. The more ambitious the program and the larger the number of voters who will benefit from it, the smaller, of course, will be the danger that Congress will risk a refusal to provide funds to finance the economic security benefits. But the danger remains.

What then can be done if we desire the federal government to participate in the social insurance method of providing economic security and the Supreme Court declares the present Act unconstitutional? All or a part of the Security Act may be declared unconstitutional because the Court disapproves of the form of the Act rather than of its underlying purposes. The decision might then provide some insight into what the Court would regard as constitutionally acceptable, and it might be possible to rewrite the Act in accordance with its requirements.

The Court would be more likely to accept the Act in a modified form if the popular reaction to their first decision revealed a strong public desire for this kind of legislation. The judges of the Supreme Court are, after all, more than nine narrow legalists: they are a group of statesmen. Mr. Justice Brandeis said many years ago that if the difference of opinion between the country as a whole and the nine judges who compose the bench as to what is socially desirable becomes too wide and persists too long, there is a real danger that the average man's respect for the constitutional system will be undermined. The judges are aware of this danger. Dissatisfaction with administration of the law was widespread in the years just before the war, and was due in large measure to failure of the Court to keep pace with the rapid development of contemporary political, economic, and social ideals. When the Court brought its ideas of legal rights more into keeping with the ordinary man's idea of social justice, it safeguarded its prestige. The Supreme Court has shown that it is prepared to take account of many considerations formerly disregarded. It has taken increasing account of state legislation as an indication of the types of legislation for which there is a general public demand. The judges may, therefore, be influenced in their attitude to the aims of the Social Security Act by their understanding of the kind of legislation generally demanded by the people of the United States.

Amendment of the Constitution

Should the Supreme Court disapprove of the Social Security Act so completely that it would not be possible by any formal changes to utilize the powers of the federal government in this field, a new clause to the Constitution specifically empowering the federal government to legislate for social security would be the only alternative.

Amending the Constitution is, of course, a cumbrous and difficult process. The amendment would have to be worded with immense care in order not to open the door to an unintended expansion of federal power. It will be difficult to draft an amendment which will give the federal government the necessary powers and yet leave the states free to deal with their own domestic affairs. But the problem, though difficult, should not prove insuperable to lawyers and social scientists. The really formidable task will be to persuade the people of America that such an amendment is essential if they are to have a satisfactory minimum of economic security. Unless the people keenly desire this security and are convinced of the necessity of providing it in ways which the Court would consider not within the present powers of the federal government, they will not stir themselves to fight for the amendment.

In view of this necessity for vigorous public feeling, it is very unfortunate that the Act has been so written that the people of America will become aware of it first of all as taxpayers. They will receive benefits only after some years. Individuals who object to paying the tax for old-age annuities will be able to attack the Act for an initial period of five years during which nobody will feel directly what is at stake because no one

228

will have received an annuity. Many people will, of course, be accumulating rights during this period. But there is all the difference in the world between losing income already previously enjoyed and losing the right to something to be enjoyed after the age of sixty-five. People will fight much harder in the former case than in the latter. In the same way no unemployment benefits are payable for the first two years after any state has passed a law. During this period there will be thousands of angry taxpayers attacking the Act and few to defend it because no one will have received any tangible benefits.

Sooner or later the constitutionality of the Act is likely to be challenged. The judges of the Supreme Court, in deciding whether it falls within the constitutional powers permitted to the federal government, will undoubtedly take account of its objectives and the social desirability of the methods adopted. If they decide against the Act, the chances of persuading them to adopt a better appreciation of existing social needs or of carrying a constitutional amendment which will make such a change of attitude unnecessary will depend upon what the people at large feel to be at stake. If voters believe that the Act will greatly increase their security, and the way of financing that security commends itself to them as being just and reasonable, they will fight for their right to have such a program. But if its administration proves unwieldy or unnecessarily burdensome, or the security it provides is negligible in amount or so hedged around by conditions and qualifications that the average man feels that it comes to nothing much, no one is likely to fight to preserve it. It will be unwise, therefore, to attempt to avoid constitutional problems by making concessions on important points which may cripple the effectiveness of the program. The fight for security can be won only if there is something worth while to fight for.

Chapter Thirteen

THE WAY TO SOCIAL SECURITY

WE are now in a better position to decide whether or not the claims made for the Social Security Act are justified. Are we to agree with Secretary of Labor Perkins that the Act "provides the majority of our people with a substantial measure of security in infancy and childhood, in economic crises of their working life, and in their old age"? Or must we recognize that there is some justice in the assertions of those who attack the Act as a snare and a delusion?

The Act is undoubtedly a step toward giving greater security to millions of people. Perhaps its most important achievement is the introduction of a new kind of security. For the first time workers will be *entitled* to income when their wages cease. Both the contributory old-age annuities and the unemployment compensation system provide payments carrying no sense of degradation, no suggestion that the recipient is in any way undeserving, and no necessity to

231

reduce himself to the status of a pauper to obtain income.

In another direction also the Security Act marks a tremendous advance. It is an acceptance by the federal government of a permanent responsibility for providing a minimum of security for the average American. For the first time federal funds are available on a large scale to increase security. For the first time there is a permanent department of the federal government charged with the responsibility of exploring ways of adding to that security. This is no emergency legislation.

The Social Security Act thus represents an advance on previous conditions so great as to be one of the major events in the social history of the country. Yet it was suggested in Chapter One that social security will be achieved only when the economic security of the individual is ensured in ways that commend themselves to the masses of the community as being just and fair and which disturb the smooth running of the economic order as little as possible. Judged by this standard the Social Security Act hardly deserves its name.

To begin with, it falls far short of providing adequate security for the individual. The need is most nearly met in the field of old-age insecurity. But even for aged people, security as a right is

limited to about one-third of the adult population. Unemployed workers will receive at best
benefits of a certain amount for only a few weeks,
and only in states passing the necessary acts.
Mothers and young children will obtain medical
advice and some treatment. The blind may
obtain higher pensions in some states, and the
disabled will be more adequately guided and
trained for new work. But the mass of adult
workers is no more secure from the economic
risks of sickness than before the Act. Needy
orphans will benefit only in states passing laws
approved by the Social Security Board. And
unless they are over sixty-five widows have little
to be thankful for.

The methods of sharing out the costs of providing even this measure of security will scarcely
command general approval when they are more
widely understood. Is it fair that young workers
and those earning less than $3,000 a year should
pay for the unearned annuities of those already
old when the Security Act was passed? If some
old people are to be given security for which they
have not paid because the Social Security Act
was not passed many years ago, would it not be
fairer that the price of this delay should be
shared among all members of the community,
rather than thrown upon those in the lower
income brackets?

The self-sustaining insurance principle, enticing as it seems at first sight, also distributes the cost of security in a way that many will question, and, in addition, has certain objectionable economic consequences. The reserve created to avoid the necessity of a contribution from federal funds will be difficult to administer and politically troublesome. Unless all the states at once pass laws, unemployed workers will receive no increase in security as a result of the unemployment compensation payroll tax. If the states do not act, the only gainer will be the federal government, which is likely to receive a considerable increase in income from the new tax.

The methods of providing and financing security adopted in the Act call for vast administrative mechanisms. The old-age annuities plan requires detailed records of the earnings of each worker throughout his working life. The unemployment compensation plan compels employers, in the states that pass laws, to keep two sets of records. The method of calculating benefits also calls for highly complicated record systems to be maintained by the states. Federal-state cooperation will necessitate the keeping of two sets of governmental records of the wages paid by every employer. Adequate security against unemployment along the lines laid down in the Act can be attained only if there are reciprocal arrangements between each of the 48 states and also close relationships between each of them and the federal government. It is not surprising that many of those who sympathize with the objects of the Act fear lest the whole security program break down beneath the weight of this administrative machinery.

It is evident that the Social Security Act, while marking the end of one chapter, is thus only the opening of another. It is unreasonable to expect to solve the whole problem of insecurity at a single blow. Even the countries more experienced in dealing with these problems have found it necessary to build up their systems slowly, improving and correcting them year by year. For many years to come (the Supreme Court willing) the Social Security Act must be the base from which amending and improving operations are conducted.

What then can be done to obtain a more socially satisfactory security? The obvious first step is to get out of the Social Security Act all that it has to give. Apart from the contributory old-age annuities plan and the grants to the United States Public Health Service, no individual can benefit from the provisions of the Act unless his state passes the necessary laws. The immediate program, therefore, is action within the states, to make the utmost possible use of the help offered by the federal government. State laws must be passed providing for old-age pensions, mothers' pensions, and the other kinds of security provided for in the Security Act. Legislators must be pressed to adjust laws already passed to the conditions laid down by the federal government.

The fullest realization of the potentialities of the Security Act depends also upon powerful popular support of the Social Security Board. This Board is destined to become one of the most influential of all the federal departments. It will administer all the most important sections of the Security Act. It will directly manage the old-age annuities plan and have the final word in approving state plans for old-age and blind pensions, unemployment compensation, and aid to dependent children. It may inherit the administration of the residual relief system. Its functions are even more comprehensive. It has been given the task of "studying and making recommendations as to the most effective methods of providing economic security through social insurance, and as to legislation and matters of administrative policy concerning old-age pensions, unemployment compensation, accident compensation and related subjects." Few public bodies can ever have been charged with so fateful a mandate.

236

It is not too much to say that the Social
Security Board can make or mar present and
future security programs. The membership of
the Board is, therefore, of vital concern to all
those who work for greater social security.
Presidents who make the appointments by and
with the consent of the Senate must be made to
feel that the country will not tolerate the appointment of inferior men or women for political
or personal reasons. The duties of the Board are
of such importance that watchfulness is needed
to prevent the Board from being crippled by
lack of funds. Had voters realized the importance
of the Board they would doubtless have compelled the 1935 Congress to appropriate funds
to enable it to carry out its tremendous duties,
instead of allowing it to face its difficult first year
of existence with no income. The Act can be a
first step toward social security only if such
financial starvation is prevented in the future.

Socially satisfactory security, however, calls
for more than state action and support for an
effective Social Security Board. The Act itself
must be amended at the earliest possible opportunity. Some amendments can properly be
demanded as carrying out the principles already
embodied in the Act. The unemployment compensation tax should be changed so as to embrace
all employers in the trades covered, regardless

of the number of workers employed by each. It should be paid not on the entire payroll but upon the wages of workers earning up to a certain sum. Workers in non-profit-making concerns should at once be placed on an equality with their fellows working for profit-making employers, and brought within the scope of the old-age annuities and unemployment compensation plans. As soon as the Social Security Board has laid the foundations of its administrative procedures, the remaining employees excluded from the old-age annuities and unemployment compensation plans should be included. The clumsy and roundabout tax offset method should be replaced by the more convenient and constitutional grant-in-aid method of returning to the states, for unemployment compensation purposes, the money collected by the federal payroll tax from their employers. None of these changes involves any serious challenge to deeply held convictions.

The major shortcomings of the Act, however, can never be remedied until we have the courage to abandon the naïve but seductive illusion that economic and social evils can be corrected without pain. We must ask ourselves how far we are prepared to sacrifice some measure of flexibility and adaptability in the economic order. Unless we are willing to pay this price, it is inconsistent to urge more adequate benefits or unemployment compensation for more than 12 or 15 weeks without pressure to take jobs at less than prevailing wages. Unless we are prepared to run some risk of rewarding the economically undeserving, we cannot urge upon the states more generous old-age pension laws. Unless we are willing to revise our views as to the proper fields of government activity, it is useless to urge that security for the unemployed should take the form of the offer of a job instead of a cash payment calling for no reciprocal service.

Criticism of the Act for providing less than adequate social security should also be made only after we have faced some additional heartsearching questions. We must be prepared to decide unequivocally who *ought* to pay for increased economic security. Unless we are willing to say, in view of the existing inequality of incomes and the low level of those at the bottom of the scale, that the richer must pay for part of the security of the poorer, it is illogical to demand revision of the financial methods of the Security Act. It is useless to urge the abandonment of the unwieldy reserve in the old-age annuities plan unless we are willing to supply from general taxation the sum that would otherwise be yielded by interest on the reserve. Are those who demand adequate security for the individual, and, at the same time complain that the taxes on employers will impose a crippling burden on productive enterprise, prepared to raise more money from general taxation? If not, the choice is between a lesser measure of security and the present taxes. Only by recognizing that the incomes of a large proportion of the population are too low to permit them to pay for their own economic security can we hope to amend the Act so as to provide adequate security in a manner that will generally be regarded as just and fair.

In the third place, we must decide how far we are prepared to sacrifice some measure of state autonomy in order to obtain more adequate social security. The demand that all Americans shall be given an equal chance of a minimum of economic security can be granted only if the federal government is given a freer hand in establishing federal security programs and setting minimum standards to be satisfied by states obtaining federal help. Unless we are prepared to take this step we cannot propose that in return for federal assistance Congress should require that the states provide pensions to the aged, the young, and the blind, sufficient to provide a minimum standard of living compatible with health and decency; nor can we write into the law a requirement that the states should insist on civil service standards in appointing their staffs to administer this vast program. So long as we refuse to modify our ideas of states rights to any degree, we cannot improve the unemployment compensation provisions by requiring that while the states may select whatever type of plan they desire, all insured workers shall be guaranteed a prescribed minimum degree of security, for at least a certain period.

Some of the worst faults of the present unemployment compensation plan, its failure to cover workers employed in more than one state, its administrative complexity, and the necessity for the collection of tremendous federal taxes with no assurance that more than a small number of the unemployed will obtain additional security, are inevitable so long as we insist that this first line of defense against unemployment must be organized on a state basis. If we are unwilling to allow the federal government to set up a national plan we must accept the shortcomings and inconveniences of the federal-state method adopted in the Social Security Act.

These are admittedly difficult choices. But we shall make no progress toward greater social security until we have squarely faced the issues. A further step is required of those who have done so, and are consciously prepared to sacrifice some measure of adaptability and flexibility in the

241

economic order, some degree of state autonomy, and (for those in the middle and higher income brackets) some measure of personal income, in order to obtain more adequate social security. They must persuade others to make similar sacrifices. Only the pressure of a powerful public opinion concerning these deeper social values can bring about changes in the law. Public opinion can be effective only when its power is felt by Congress.

The Social Security Act may be inadequate, it may be complicated, and its methods of sharing out the cost of security may well be regarded by many as unfair. In the last analysis, however, these shortcomings are attributable to our own lack of clarity as to what we want and the price we are prepared to pay to attain our objective. Until we have faced these fundamental issues and are prepared to accept the sacrifice they involve, it is unreasonable to expect a more satisfactory Act. We hand over to busy Congressmen the task of working out a law to provide social security and we fail to give them any guidance on the most essential and difficult points, namely, those involving our willingness to sacrifice cherished illusions. In short, "the fault, dear Brutus, lies not in our stars but in ourselves."

Appendix

SUMMARY OF PROVISIONS OF THE FEDERAL SOCIAL SECURITY ACT RELATING TO FEDERAL OLD-AGE BENEFITS AND FEDERAL EMPLOYMENT TAXES

(Public No. 271, 74th Cong. [H. R. 7260]; Approved
Aug. 14, 1935)

Issued by the Social Security Board

FEDERAL OLD-AGE BENEFITS (TITLE II)

Coverage (Sec. 210*b*)

Old-age benefits are to be paid to all employees based upon wages received in employment in any service performed within the United States, Alaska and Hawaii except:

1. Agricultural labor,
2. Domestic service in a private home,
3. Casual labor not in the course of employer's trade or business,
4. Officers or members of the crew of a vessel documented under the laws of the United States or of any foreign country,
5. Employees of the United States Government,
6. Employees of a state or political subdivision,
7. Employees of nonprofit institutions operated exclusively for religious, charitable, scientific,

243

literary, or educational purposes, or for the prevention of cruelty to children or animals,

8. Employees of a carrier as defined in Railroad Retirement Act of 1935 (Public No. 399, 74th Cong. [H.R. 8651]).

Conditions to Qualify for Receipt of Old-age Benefits (Sec. 210c)

1. At least sixty-five years of age,
2. Not less than $2,000 total wages received after December 31, 1936, and before age of sixty-five,
3. Wages were paid to individual on some day in each of five years after December 31, 1936, and before age of sixty-five.

Old-age Benefit Payments (Sec. 202)

1. Date first payable—January 1, 1942.
2. The amount of the monthly benefits payable is determined as follows:

Total wages received after December 31, 1936, and prior to age sixty-five, in covered employments	Per cent of total wages paid as monthly benefit
Not counting wages in excess of $3,000 annually.	
First $ 3,000	½ per cent
Next 42,000	1⁄12 per cent
All over 45,000	1⁄24 per cent

244

3. Illustrative benefits are as follows:

Average monthly salary	Years of employment			
	10	20	30	40
$ 50	$17.50	$22.50	$27.50	$32.50
100	22.50	32.50	42.50	51.25
150	27.50	42.50	53.75	61.25
200	32.50	51.25	61.25	71.25
250	37.50	56.25	68.75	81.25

Minimum monthly benefit, $10; maximum, $85.

4. Non-qualified individuals upon reaching age of sixty-five are paid a lump sum equal to $3\frac{1}{2}$ per cent of the total wages paid after December 31, 1936, and before the attainment of age sixty-five (Sec. 204).

5. Upon death of individual before age of sixty-five, his estate receives payment equal to $3\frac{1}{2}$ per cent of his total wages received after December 31, 1936; if he dies after age of sixty-five, his estate receives the same amount less any benefits paid to him during his lifetime (Sec. 208).

6. Payment of benefit withheld for each month in which a qualified individual who has attained age sixty-five received wages for regular employment (Sec. 202d).

7. Payments not subject to assignment or other legal process (Sec. 208).

Federal Administration

Old-age Reserve Account in the U. S. Treasury. The Secretary of the Treasury submits annual estimate to Budget of appropriation to be made to account; and invests funds which draw interest at 3 per cent (Sec. 201).

Social Security Board determines the qualifications of the individual and amount of benefits payable (Sec. 202*a*); certifies to Treasury persons entitled to payments (Sec. 207).

FEDERAL TAXES WITH RESPECT TO EMPLOYMENT (TITLE VIII)

Coverage (Sec. 811*b*)

Federal taxes are to be paid by all employers and employees based on wages received in employment in any service performed within the United States, Alaska and Hawaii except:

1. Agricultural labor,
2. Domestic service in a private home,
3. Casual labor not in the course of employer's trade or business,
4. An individual who has attained sixty-five years,
5. Officers or members of the crew of a vessel documented under the laws of the United States or of any foreign country,
6. Employees of the United States government,
7. Employees of a state or a political subdivision,
8. Employees of nonprofit institutions operated exclusively for religious, charitable, scientific, literary, or educational purposes, or for the prevention of cruelty to children or animals,

9. Employees of a carrier as defined in (Public No. 400, 74th Cong. [H.R. 8652]).

Rates of Taxes

Taxes assessed on wages not counting in excess of $3,000 annually paid any individual (Sec. 811*a*).

INCOME TAX ON WAGES OF EMPLOYEES (SEC. 801)

Calendar year	Tax
1937, 1938, and 1939	1 per cent
1940, 1941, and 1942	1½ per cent
1943, 1944, and 1945	2 per cent
1946, 1947, and 1948	2½ per cent
1949 and thereafter	3 per cent

Income tax on employee collected by employer by deducting the tax from wages (Sec. 802*a*). But such a tax not to be allowed as a deduction in computing net income for Income Tax purposes (Sec. 803).

EXCISE TAX ON WAGES PAID BY EMPLOYERS (SEC. 804)

Calendar year	Tax
1937, 1938, and 1939	1 per cent
1940, 1941, and 1942	1½ per cent
1943, 1944, and 1945	2 per cent
1946, 1947, and 1948	2½ per cent
1949 and thereafter	3 per cent

Federal Administration

Taxes collected by Bureau of Internal Revenue under direction of Secretary of Treasury and paid into United States Treasury as internal-revenue collections (Sec. 807*a*). Commissioner of Internal Revenue with approval of Secretary of Treasury makes rules for enforcement of title (Sec. 808).

Taxes collected in such manner, at such time, and under such conditions (either by making and filing returns or by stamps, coupons, tickets, books, or other reasonable devices or methods) as may be prescribed by the Commissioner of Internal Revenue, who furnishes to the Postmaster General a suitable quantity to be kept at post offices. The Postmaster General at least once a month transfers to Treasury as internal-revenue collections all receipts so deposited (Sec. 809).

SUMMARY OF PROVISIONS OF THE FEDERAL SOCIAL SECURITY ACT RELATING TO UNEMPLOYMENT COMPENSATION

(Public No. 271, 74th Cong. [H.R. 7260]; Approved Aug. 14, 1935)

Issued by the Social Security Board

To be administered by the Social Security Board established by Title VII of the Act

FEDERAL GRANTS TO STATES FOR ADMINISTRATION OF UNEMPLOYMENT COMPENSATION (TITLE III)

Amount of Federal Appropriation Authorized (Sec. 301)

Fiscal year ending June 30, 1936—$ 4,000,000.
Fiscal years thereafter   — 49,000,000.

Amount of Grant to Each State (Sec. 302a)

Such amount granted from time to time as the Social Security Board determines to be necessary for the proper administration of the state law during the fiscal year in which payment is to be made, taking into account:

1. Population of the state;
2. Number of persons covered by the state law and the cost of proper administration thereof;
3. Such other factors as the Social Security Board finds relevant.

The Secretary of the Treasury upon receipt of certification of the Social Security Board shall pay prior to audit

249

or settlement by the General Accounting Office the amount certified to the state agency charged with the administration of the law.

The Social Security Board shall not certify payments in excess of the amount appropriated for any fiscal year.

State Matching Required

None.

Required Provisions of State Unemployment Compensation Administration for receipt of Federal Grants (Sec. 303a)

1. Approval of state law by Social Security Board under title IX.

2. "Such methods of administration (other than those relating to selection, tenure of office, and compensation of personnel) as are found by the Board to be reasonably calculated to insure full payment of unemployment compensation when due; and

3. "Payment of unemployment compensation solely through public employment offices in the state or such other agencies as the Board may approve; and

4. "Opportunity for a fair hearing, before an impartial tribunal, for all individuals whose claims for unemployment compensation are denied; and

5. "The payment of all money received in the unemployment fund of such state, immediately upon such receipt, to the Secretary of the Treasury to the credit of the Unemployment Trust Fund established by section 904; and

6. "Expenditure of all money requisitioned by the state agency from the Unemployment Trust Fund, in the payment of unemployment compensation, exclusive of expenses of administration; and

7. "The making of such reports, in such form and containing such information, as the Board may from time to time require, and compliance with such provisions as the Board may from time to time find necessary to assure the correctness and verification of such reports;" and

8. Making available upon request to any federal agency administering public works or assistance through public employment, the name, address, occupation, employment status and rights to further compensation of each recipient of unemployment compensation.

Suspension of Grants (Sec. 303b)

If the Social Security Board finds, after reasonable notice and opportunity for hearing to the state agency, either (1) that a substantial number of persons entitled to compensation are being denied compensation, or (2) that the state has failed to comply substantially with the provisions required in section 303a, the Board shall notify such state agency that further payment will not be made until the Board is satisfied that there is no longer any such denial or failure to comply.

FEDERAL TAX UPON EMPLOYERS OF EIGHT OR MORE EMPLOYEES (TITLE IX)

Coverage of Federal Tax (Sec. 907)

Employers of eight or more individuals employed on each of some 20 days in year, each day being in a different calendar week, in employments performed within the United States, except the following employments:

1. Agricultural labor;
2. Domestic service in a private home;

3. Officer or member of the crew of a vessel on the navigable waters of the United States.

4. Individual in the employ of son, daughter, or spouse; child under 21 years in employ of his parent;

5. Public employees—federal, state and local;

6. Employees of nonprofit institutions operated exclusively for religious, charitable, scientific, literary, or educational purposes, or for the prevention of cruelty to children or animals.

Rate of Tax on Employers (Sec. 901)

1 per cent of wages paid in 1936; 2 per cent in 1937; 3 per cent thereafter.

Credit Allowed for Payments under State Unemployment Compensation Law

1. Not to exceed 90 per cent of federal tax. (Sec. 902)

2. After 1937 additional credit is also allowable to any employer who because of favorable employment experience or adequate reserves is permitted by the state law to reduce his payments, subject to the following conditions (Sec. 910):

(a) If the employer contributes to a state pooled fund, the lower rate is based upon not less than three years' compensation experience.

(b) If the employer contributes to a guaranteed employment account, the lower rate is permitted only if the guaranty was fulfilled during the preceding year and the account amounts to not less than 7½ per cent of total wages paid during the preceding calendar year.

(c) If the employer contributes to a separate reserve account, the lower rate is permitted only if (1) compensation has been payable from the account throughout the preceding calendar year, (2) the account amounts to not less than five times the largest amount of compensation paid during any one of the three preceding calendar years, and (3) such account amounts to 7½ per cent of the wages paid during the preceding year.

Required Provisions of State Unemployment Compensation Law for Allowance of Credit (Sec. 903*a*)

1. All compensation to be paid through public employment offices in the state or such other agencies as the Board may approve;

2. No compensation to be payable until after two years after contributions first required;

3. State unemployment fund to be deposited with the Unemployment Trust Fund of the U. S. Treasury;

4. Money withdrawn from the Unemployment Trust Fund to be used solely for unemployment compensation, exclusive of administrative expenses;

5. Compensation not to be denied any eligible individual for refusal to accept work if (a) the position vacant is due directly to a strike, lockout, or labor dispute, (b) the wages, hours, or conditions of work are substantially less favorable to the individual than those prevailing in the locality, or (c) if the individual would be required to join a company union or to resign from or refrain from joining a bona fide labor organization;

6. State must retain the right to repeal or amend its law.

Revocation of Approval of State Plans (Sec. 903*b*)

The Social Security Board may, at end of any year after reasonable notice and opportunity for hearing, refuse to certify a state whose plan has been previously approved in case the state law has been changed so that it no longer contains the above conditions, or if the state has failed to comply substantially with these conditions. If at any time the Board has reason to believe a state law may not be certified it shall promptly notify the Governor.

Unemployment Trust Fund (Sec. 904)

All moneys received in the state unemployment fund must be deposited in the Unemployment Trust Fund maintained by the United States Treasury, subject to requisition of the state. These funds are invested by the Treasury and bear interest at the average rate paid by the United States upon all interest-bearing obligations. A separate account is maintained for each state.

Interstate Commerce (Sec. 906)

No person required by state law to make payments to an unemployment compensation fund shall be relieved on the ground that he is engaged in interstate commerce, or that the state law does not distinguish between employees engaged in interstate and intrastate commerce.

*Summary of Provisions of the Social Security
Act Relating to Federal Grants to States*

SUMMARY OF PROVISIONS OF THE SOCIAL SECURITY

(Public No. 271, 74th Cong.

Provision	Old-age assistance (Secs. 1–6)	Aid to the blind (Secs. 1001–1006)	Aid to dependent children (Secs. 401–406)
Conditions for approval of state plan.	1. A state plan (for each type of assistance, aid, or service) must be federal administrative agency for approval. For old-age assistance, aid to the blind, and aid to dependent children, each of the plans must be state-wide, and, if administered by political subdivisions, must be mandatory upon them. 2. Financial participation by the state must be provided in the state service). A state old-age assistance plan need not provide state financial participation before July 1, 1937, where the Board finds the state is so prevented by its constitution. 3. A single state agency must be established or designated to administer to supervise the administration of the state plan. 4. Methods of administration (other than those relating to select necessary for the efficient operation of the plan. 5. Reports must be submitted in such form and containing such required by the designated federal administrative agency. 6. Persons whose claims for assistance have been denied must be permitted an opportunity for a fair hearing before the state agency. 7. State residence requirement may not exceed 5 years within last 9 years. One year of residence immediately preceding application may be required. 8. A state plan cannot impose any citizenship requirement which excludes any United States citizen. 9. After January 1, 1940, state plan must provide an age limit of not over 65 years, but until then a 70-year limit is permissible. 10. One-half of any recovery from estate of a recipient to be paid to the United States.	9. No aid to be given blind person while in receipt of old-age assistance under a federally approved plan.	7. State residence requirement must not disqualify a child who has resided in the state for a year immediately preceding application, or who was born in the state during the preceding year, if its mother has resided in the state for one year immediately preceding the birth.

APPENDIX

ACT RELATING TO FEDERAL GRANTS TO STATES
H.R. 7260]; Approved Aug. 14, 1935)

Maternal and child health (Secs. 501–505)	Crippled children (Secs. 511–515)	Child welfare (Sec. 521)	Public health (Secs. 601–603)
submitted by the state to the designated		The conditions are those involved in the purposes of the section: To enable the United States to cooperate with the states in establishing, extending, and strengthening, in predominantly rural areas, child-welfare services for the protection and care of homeless, dependent, and neglected children, and children in danger of becoming delinquent. The amounts shall be allotted on the basis of plans developed jointly by the Children's Bureau and state public-welfare agencies and be expended for payment of part of the cost of local services in areas predominantly rural, and for developing state services for the encouragement and assistance of adequate methods of community child-welfare organization in areas predominantly rural and other areas of special need.	The conditions are those involved in the purposes of the act, which are to assist states "in establishing and maintaining adequate public-health services, including the training of personnel for state and local health work." The moneys paid to any state must be used solely in carrying out these purposes and in accordance with plans presented by the state health authority to the Public Health Service.
plan (for each type of assistance, aid or			
minister the state plan or established or designated			
For maternal and child-health services the state health agency must be used.			
ion, tenure, and compensation of personnel)			
nformation as may be from time to time			
6. Provide for the extension and improvement of local maternal and child-health services administered by local child-health units.	6. Provide for carrying out the purposes specified in the appropriation.		
7. Provide for cooperation with medical, nursing, and welfare groups and organizations.	7. Provide cooperation with medical, health, nursing, and welfare organizations and with agencies charged with vocational rehabilitation of physically handicapped children.		
8. Provide for development of demonstration services in needy areas and among groups in special need.			

SUMMARY OF PROVISIONS OF THE SOCIAL SECURITY ACT

Provision	Old-age assistance (Secs. 1–6)	Aid to the blind (Secs. 1001–1006)	Aid to dependent children (Secs. 401–406)
Amount of federal grant to state.	One-half of state expenditures for assistance under each plan; but payments in excess of $30 a month to an individual are not matched by federal government. Five per cent of federal aid to state for administration and/or assistance under each plan.		One-third of state expenditures; but payments in excess of $18 per month for first child and $12 for each additional child are not matched by federal government.
Extent of state financial participation.	Amount equal to federal payment to state exclusive of federal 5 per cent.		Amount double federal payment to state.
Federal definition of aid.	Money payments to needy individual 65 years or older not an inmate of public institution.	Money payments to needy blind individual not an inmate of a public institution.	Money payments to needy dependent child or children under 16 years by reason of death, absence, or incapacity of a parent, living with an enumerated relative in a residence maintained as a home.
Method of making allotments.	Allotments made for each quarter on the basis of estimated state gations by the appropriate federal agency. Payments made to the state (at time or times fixed by the desigsion) prior to audit or settlement by the General Accounting Office.		
Suspension of federal grant.	In the case of an approved plan which the Board finds after reasonable notice and opportunity for hearing has been changed to impose a prohibited requirement; or in the administration imposes a prohibited requirement with the knowledge of the state agency in a substantial number of cases, or fails to comply substantially with the provisions required in the plan, the Board shall notify the state agency that further payments will not be made.		
Federal agency	Social Security Board	Social Security Board	Social Security Board
Federal appropriation authorized—Fiscal year 1936.	$49,750,000	$3,000,000	$24,750,000

NOTE.—The Social Security Act also authorizes in Sec. 531 an appropriation of $841,-
tation purposes, in addition to the appropriation available under the provisions of existing
n the Department of the Interior. The Social Security Act also authorizes in Title III an
states for the administration of their unemployment compensation laws.

APPENDIX

Maternal and child health (Secs. 501–505)	Crippled children (Secs. 511–515)	Child welfare (Sec. 521)	Public health (Secs. 601–603)
$20,000 to each state; and $1,800,000 distributed to the states in proportion to live births; and $980,000 distributed on basis of need, taking into consideration number of live births in state.	$20,000 allotted to each state and $1,830,000 distributed to the states on the basis of need taking into consideration the number of crippled children in need of such services and the cost thereof.	$10,000 alloted to each of the states and $990,000 distributed to the states not to exceed proportion of state to United States rural population.	$8,000,000 distributed to the states on the basis of (1) population, (2) special health problems, (3) financial needs.
Amount equal to federal payment to state exclusive of allotment on basis of need.	Amount equal to federal payment.	Not specifically provided in act.	Not specifically provided in act.
Services for promoting the health of mothers and children.	Services and facilities for crippled children or for children suffering from conditions whch lead to crippling.	See above under "Conditions for approval of state plan."	See above under "Conditions for approval of state plan."
expenditures and appropriations, and investi-		Not specifically provided in act.	Allotments made for each quarter in accordance with regulations previously prescribed after conference with state health authorities.
nated federal agency) by the Secretary of the Treasury (through Disbursement Divi-			
In the case of an approved plan which the Secretary of Labor finds after reasonable notice and opportunity for hearing fails to comply substantially in the administration of the plan the Secretary shall notify the state agency that further payments will not be made.		Not specifically provided in act.	Not specifically provided in act.
Children's Bureau	Children's Bureau	Children's Bureau	Public Health Service
$3,800,000	$2,850,000	$1,500,000	$8,000,000

000 for the fiscal year 1936, to be distributed as grants to the states for vocational rehabililaw; the Federal Vocational Rehabilitation Act is administered by the Office of Education appropriation of $4,000,000 for the fiscial year 1936, to be distributed as grants to the

INDEX

261